THE GAMBLERS

John Pearson's career as a biographer includes books on the Churchills, the Windsors, the Gettys and the Sitwells. He has also written an award-winning travel book on Timbuctoo, a bestselling biography of Ian Fleming and the authorised biography of James Bond. However, he is probably best known for his two in-depth studies of the Kray Twins, and is currently working on the final part of his Kray trilogy.

Praise for *The Gamblers*:

'Riveting book . . . Pearson cleverly switches from a group biography into a murder mystery and, because he concentrates on Lucan's disappearance, rather than the more well-known facts about the killing of the nanny in the Belgravia basement, he entices the reader into a whodunnit. The gripping depiction of this amoral hierarchy sets John Pearson's book apart' *Independent on Sunday*

'with remarkable candour, Pearson's sources have told him how members of the Clermont set helped Lucan plan the murder of his wife, and he has come up with fascinating new evidence of Lucan's escape after it went wrong. By mistake Lucan killed his family nanny and fled . . . a remarkable scoop and it makes a riveting and very plausible twist in the story.' Adam Curtis, *The Oldie*

'G̶e̶n̶u̶i̶n̶e̶ M̶a̶y̶fair noir thriller' *Sunday Times*

'Pearson̶ . . . L̶ucan's fate . . . *Mail*

Also available by John Pearson

Non-fiction

Bluebird and the Dead Lake
The Persuasion Industry (with Graham Turner)
The Life of Ian Fleming
Arena: The Story of the Colosseum
The Profession of Violence
Edward the Rake
Façades: Edith, Osbert and Sacheverell Sitwell
Stags and Serpents: The Cavendish Dukes of Devonshire
The Ultimate Family: The Making of the House of
Windsor
Citadel of the Heart: Winston and the Churchill Dynasty
Painfully Rich: J. Paul Getty and His Heirs
Blood Royal: The Story of the Spencers and the Royals
The Cult of Violence
One of the Family: The Englishman and the Mafia

Fiction

Gone to Timbuctoo
The Life of James Bond
The Kindness of Dr Avicenna

JOHN PEARSON

THE GAMBLERS

arrow books

Published in the United Kingdom by Arrow Books in 2007

9 10 8

Copyright © John Pearson 2005

John Pearson has asserted his right under the Copyright, Designs and
Patents Act, 1988 to be identified as the author of this work

First published in the United Kingdom in 2005 by Century

Arrow Books
The Random House Group Limited
20 Vauxhall Bridge Road, London, SW1V 2SA

Addresses for companies within The Random House Group Limited
can be found at: www.randomhouse.co.uk

The Random House Group Limited Reg. No. 954009

A CIP catalogue record for this book
is available from the British Library

ISBN 9780099461180

Penguin Random House is committed to a sustainable future for
our business, our readers and our planet. This book is made from
Forest Stewardship Council® certified paper.

Typeset by SX Composing DTP, Rayleigh, Essex

Printed and bound in Great Britain by Clays Ltd, St Ives plc

Contents

For Lynette,
Yet again – and for ever.

'I have a notion that Gamblers are as happy as most people being always *excited*. Women, wine, fame, the table, even Ambition, *sate* now and then; but every turn of the card, and cast of the dice, keeps the gamester alive: besides, one can game ten times longer than one can do anything else'

Lord Byron

'All of life is six–four against'

Damon Runyon

Acknowledgements

When I started working on this book, I saw it as a chronicle of the rise and fall of the so-called Clermont Set and, as such, a fascinating part of the social history of the Sixties and early Seventies. Certainly the last thing I foresaw was getting involved in the story of what did or didn't happen to Lord Lucan. But books have a strange way of asserting an existence of their own, and quite early on in my research I began to realise how profoundly that mysterious event came to dominate the lives of those around him. More than that it was obviously so bound up with the weird conclusion of my story that I had to take account of it. In the process, I reached what I believed to be the closest we will ever get to answering this enduring mystery.

But I must emphasize that the original purpose of this book remains, and I like to think that it is something more than a simple murder mystery. I can only say that in writing it I became fascinated by the lives and the obsessions of an extraordinary group bound so powerfully together by the everlasting force of gambling – and much besides.

In the process I was helped by many who have helped me. Among them I would like to thank Anthony Alfrey, Lady Sally Aspinall, Sir David Attenborough, Al Alvarez, Melissa Bakewell, John Burke, Mark Birley, Robin Birley, Richard Compton Miller, Sarah Carr, Willie Donaldson, Peter Elwes, James Fox, Walter Felgate, Michael Gillard, Anne Halsey, Roy Houghton, Sue Hunt, Max Hastings, Richard Ingrams, Tessa Kennedy, Louis Jebb, Sir Dai Llewellyn, Anthony Little, the late David Leitch, Dominick Midgley, the late Susie Maxwell-Scott, George Monbiot, Euan Macleod, Lord Oaksey, James Osborne, Helen Pennant-Rea, James Saunders, Archie Stirling, Taki Theodoracopulos, Jane Telling, Tim Thomas, Hugo Vickers, George Valentini, Margaret Vyner, Melissa Wyndham, and Athena Zographos.

Among others who have made this book possible, I must also thank my director of studies, Wendie McWatters, my agent Michael Sissons, my publisher, Mark Booth and his heroic assistant, Kate Watkins and Amanda Russell. Brian Eke has saved my sanity over my computer, Hugh

acknowledgements

Bashaarat has been endlessly kind and under-standing, and Ted Green, though very old, has been always there when I needed him. Edda Tasiemka and her magical archive has as ever been a wondrous source of information.

Lastly I must thank my wife, Lynette, who has helped, endured, and contributed more to the writing of this book than she will ever know.

1

Gone With the Wind

'YOU REMEMBER *Gone With the Wind*?' said Dai Llewellyn. He was in reminiscent mode, as he often is these days. I nodded.

'You may recall that following the opening credits, two sentences were flashed upon the screen explaining what the film was all about. "A civilisation vanished overnight. Everything gone with the wind." Since you ask, that's how I feel about the Clermont Club and the Lucky Lucan episode. It wasn't just the murder of the nanny Sandra Rivett and what did or didn't happen to Lucky afterwards. I knew him, of course. Quite well. Used to play backgammon with him. Good backgammon player, but I can't say I liked him. Never had. Dull dog. Drank too much, but that was not the point. Nor was it whether he had or hadn't killed the unfortunate nanny. For me what counted was that from the moment of the murder, everything that had made the Clermont Club unique vanished. Not just the gambling but the people, and a way of life, all suddenly swept away.

'I remember coming here in the afternoon after it occurred. The murder was already making front-page headlines in the early editions of the evening papers, and this whole place, which was normally buzzing with people after lunch, was empty as a sinking ship. Few of them returned. A society, and a very interesting one, had gone with the wind.'

★

When all this happened back in November 1974, the handsome young Dai Llewellyn was social secretary of the Clermont Club in Berkeley Square. The baronet son of the Olympic champion showjumper, Sir Harry Llewellyn, and brother of Roddy Llewellyn, Princess Margaret's lover, he remains a bon viveur, a confirmed gambler, and a great survivor. Now, thirty years later, he was taking me to see the club as it is today to watch the gambling.

Even to me it was obvious at once that this was a very different world from the one that he remembered. The dinner-jacketed croupiers, most of them trained in France, had long since gone. In their place impassive girls in black silk dresses dealt out coloured gaming counters, paid the winners and raked back the losers' counters for the house. *Chemin de fer*, the trademark game of the old Clermont, which brought debt and misery to so many members of the English aristocracy, had long since disappeared. In place of the 'shoe', which held eight packs of playing cards and used to make its solemn way around the table under the eagle eye of the croupier, there was now the effortless rotation of the roulette wheel. Nor did one hear the cries of 'banco' or 'suivi', as the chemmy players bellowed out their bids. Modern high-stakes gambling is a silent and profoundly serious business.

The most noticeable feature of big, present-day gambling clubs like the modern Clermont is their extraordinary discretion. In the days that Dai remembered, the great gambling room at the Clermont was usually crammed with grandees and celebrities These days the true high rollers are so anonymous and self-effacing that it would be hard to pick them out. I mentioned this to Dai.

'I doubt you'd recognise them. Anyhow, when any serious gambling is going on these days, it usually takes place in a private room. Today the very rich don't advertise the fact.'

What hasn't changed at the Clermont is that it still inhabits one of the hidden architectural treasures of the capital. The house at 44 Berkeley Square was built between 1741 and 1744 by the architect William Kent, who specialised in recreating the splendours of the palaces of Rome and the Veneto for the aristocracy of mid-eighteenth-century England. It was home to Lady Isabella 'Belle' Finch, daughter of the Earl of Winchilsea. The Earl happened to be extraordinarily rich, which was just as well, since he had six other daughters to provide for. Belle was a spinster and a lady-in-waiting to George II's daughter, Princess Amelia. As she was single, the house required only one main bedroom, and since there was no need to accommodate a family, Kent used the space as a setting for Lady Belle's passion for regal entertaining. The whole house remains pure and magnificent theatre.

Architectural historians get excited over the Clermont's unsupported staircase which is apparently a considerable technical achievement. I find it difficult to get too worked up about a staircase.

But the great, first floor salon is something that will take the breath away from all but the most obsessional gambler. The fact that Kent created it within the compass of a London terraced house has served to concentrate its impact. Had one of Belle Finch's eighteenth-century noblemen, freshly returned from the Grand Tour, fallen into a drunken stupor and, on waking, gazed up at that great coffered ceiling with its painted and richly gilded panels high above him, one could imagine him thinking he was still in Rome, and wondering whose palazzo he was in.

*

The Club's name was taken from Belle Finch's immediate successor in the house, the 1st Earl of Clermont, whose only claim to fame was to win the Derby in 1785. The Club itself was the carefully devised creation of one of the most extraordinary characters of the sixties, high priest of gamblers, showman of genius, close friend of tigers and gorillas, together with a refined taste in food, books and eighteenth-century architecture, who ended up angrily despairing of humanity. For good or ill he was a key figure in that multitudinous decade. His name was John Aspinall.

Thanks to a famous legal case in 1958 he had already done more than anyone in the previous century and a half to revolutionise the obsolete gaming laws of England. It was this, and the Gaming Act that ensued, that effectively legalised gambling clubs in Britain and turned sixties London into the gambling capital of Europe.

Within eighteen months of opening in November 1962, the Clermont's turnover was greater than that of any of the casinos in Monte Carlo, Deauville or Le Touquet, and was making John Aspinall a fortune. He ruled his club like a private fiefdom.

The secret of Aspinall's success was very simple, and not really a secret. Having seen how the easing of the gambling laws had created such a taste for gambling among the idle and richer members of society, he became the self-appointed Pied Piper of gambling to the English upper classes. He tailored the club precisely to their needs, and the Clermont soon appeared to be attracting half the members of the English aristocracy to its tables. Nothing quite like this had happened since the wild, high-rolling days of the Regency gamblers a century and a half before, and soon more dukes and earls and viscounts were visiting No. 44 than ever called on Lady Isabella Finch.

To complete the process, barely a year after opening, a gambling friend of Aspinall's, a former advertising man called Mark Birley, turned the cellars into a nightclub. Having married Lady Annabel Vane-Tempest-Stewart, the daughter of the Marquess of Londonderry, he saw no harm in reminding people of the fact, and called it Annabel's. After a slow start, Annabel's began to share in the success of the Clermont, and became the smartest and the most exclusive night club in the capital and was packing in the fashionable and famous (and the would-be fashionable and the would-be famous) from dusk till dawn. With high-stakes gambling upstairs and disco dancing down below, 44 Berkeley Square was at the forefront of a social movement that soon spread out across Swinging London.

In Downing Street, Harold Macmillan, the Scottish crofter's grandson who became son-in-law to a duke, had recently appointed more aristocrats to his cabinet than any prime minister since the war, and in Berkeley Square the rich were unashamedly proclaiming that they'd do whatever they felt like doing with their money - and their women. This blatant mix of high-stakes gambling, sophisticated sex, and the antics of what were taken to be the British upper classes was inevitably picked on by the media as proof that the British aristocracy was alive and flourishing. After years of slow decline, wealth and privilege were on the march, and this combined gaming club and nightclub in Berkeley Square, where the nightingale once sang, was their headquarters.

This alone gives 44 Berkeley Square a place in the social history of the sixties. But as well as this, there lies a story that still haunts this house. It involves the so-called Clermont Set and the five friends most closely involved in it from the beginning. Gambling had become their way of life. They lived by taking risks, and shared a code of loyalty to each other. They pretended to despise dull middle-class society, and it seemed as if through gambling they had attained everything they wanted – the smartest friends, the most beautiful women and the entrée to some of the grandest houses in the land.

In their private lives these friends had all been playing for the highest stakes for years. And as with all serious gamblers, some enjoyed enormous luck while others met with terrible disasters. The most catastrophic gamble, which finally affected all of them and destroyed the Clermont Set for ever, was that embarked on by one of the original members, Lucky Lucan. It was a gamble that not only ended in a murder, but led indirectly to the suicide of another member. In the fallout from this second death, a third important member of the group became so discredited that he left the country, moved permanently abroad, and made himself the richest gambler in the world.

As for the two key members of the Set, John Aspinall and Mark Birley, they had already fallen out and rarely spoke to one another, but in the aftermath of the murder, other unconnected events meant that by the time of Aspinall's own death any hope of eventual reconciliation had become slim. So in spite of the high hopes with which the five friends started out, and despite their original loyalty to each other, Dai Llewellyn's words rang true. After that November night, it was all gone, gone with the wind.

2

A Gambling Man
from Oxford

When John Aspinall opened the Clermont Club in 1962, he claimed to have five dukes, eight viscounts and seventeen earls on its membership list. But although he seemed entirely at home among the aristocracy, and made sure that humbler gamblers were blackballed from his club – unless they were remarkably rich – in social terms it would have been extremely hard to 'place' John Aspinall himself.

Socially speaking, he emerged from nowhere, having been born in Delhi in 1926. His father was a Maltese doctor called Stivala who changed his name to Robert Aspinall on joining the Indian Medical Service. But Dr Aspinall was not his real father. That privilege had been usurped by a young lieutenant from the Lincolnshire Regiment who according to Aspinall 'seduced my mother under a tamarisk tree beside the banks of a stream in Naimital.'

John Aspinall's strong-willed mother, Mary, was a member of an old Anglo-Indian family. She was born near Nagpur in the hot and dusty Central Provinces, and her father, a civil engineer called Horn, built bridges. At eighteen she escaped from life in provincial India by eloping with the reinvented Dr Aspinall a few weeks after meeting him. Determined young woman that she was, she made her new husband apply at once for a medical posting in Delhi, but although the doctor had a distinguished medical career in India and ended up as Surgeon General and doctor to the Viceroy, she ultimately tired of him and life in Delhi, and decided that she wanted to return to England.

Her fling with the lieutenant from the Lincoln-shires ended with his posting to West Africa, but she did not repine. She was a risk-taker and, as she showed later, an inveterate gambler. She was also very tough and a great survivor. When her marriage ended in divorce, she chanced her luck with a sympathetic colonel who had consoled her on the ship that brought her back to England. Once again her luck did not desert her. Colonel Osborne was a gentleman. He loved her, married her and would give her three more children.

Like many determined women, Mary Osborne was possessed of a cheerful manner and a homely figure. She was a devoted mother, but her favourite child was not one of her growing brood of little Osbornes. Nor was it her first-born, Dr Aspinall's one legitimate child who had been christened Robert after his father. Her love was showered on her love child, whose thick blond hair and powerful physique must have brought back memories of her lost lieutenant and romantic nights in Delhi.

Colonel and Mrs Osborne took a house near Uckfield in the heart of Sussex, and automatically assumed their place among the local gentry. By now the Colonel had discovered that, for him at any rate, the secret of a happy life lay in following the dictates of his strong-willed wife, and when she decided John must go to an English public school, he readily agreed. Some of her relations had gone to Tom Brown's alma mater, Rugby, and Dr Aspinall agreed to pay the fees. Rugby was originally set up to turn out solid citizens who would help to rule the Empire. The idea of the Empire did not particularly appeal to the young John Aspinall.

He had become a tall, good-looking boy with very pale blue eyes. A girl who saw him for the first time at a point-to-point near Steyning at around this time remembers him 'looking like the young Apollo with a halo of thick gold hair.'

Like most young gods, he was congenitally idle and, like his mother, he was sufficiently strong-willed to do exactly as he pleased. Although he was something of a loner, other boys were wary of him. So were the masters, for he had little patience with authority and, when punished, endured beatings with cool indifference. Until the age of seventeen, he managed to survive on a minimum of schoolwork. Competitive sport bored him, but in spite of this, his strength and aggressiveness earned him a place in the First XV, playing the game his school invented and to which it gave its name.

He was at an age where nothing seemed to satisfy him. To alleviate the tedium of school life, he turned to the popular adventure novels of Sir Henry Rider Haggard. Today few adolescents read Rider Haggard, but in books like his *Nada the Lily*,

Aspinall found what he was seeking in this stirring tale of Shaka, king of the Zulus. Shaka was someone he could identify with – physically courageous, proudly unconcerned with what others thought of him, tough with women, mighty in battle and unflinching in the face of disaster. Hoping to become some sort of Rider Haggard hero, John dropped what he felt to be the unexciting name he had been given, and gave himself the more exciting appellation of Jonas V. Aspinall.

By now it was becoming clear that Rugby School and Jonas V. Aspinall had little further use for one another, and when the school suggested that at seventeen the time had come for them to part, he raised no objections. He volunteered for the Royal Marines, but found army life as tedious as life at school. The war in Europe was ending, and he served nearly three years as a private in the Marines without promotion or particular distinction. Demobilised in 1948, he had no idea about his future, apart from having formed a vague desire to be a writer.

A cousin suggested that there might be worse fates for an aspiring writer than studying English Literature at Oxford. He added that, should he wish to do so, Jesus College might accept him, since its current Principal was an Old Rugbeian. For want of anything more enticing, Aspinall followed his advice, and when he applied to the college, whatever love he had for English Literature proved less important than his status as a returning serviceman who had played in Rugby's First XV.

In the autumn term of 1949, Jesus College opened its four-hundred-year-old gates to twenty-one-year-old Jonas V. Aspinall. The college and the freshman took an instantaneous dislike to one another.

He sampled the food, the company and the amenities, all of which struck him as inferior to what he had endured in the Marines. Food in Hall, still rationed at the time, was grim, and he was expected to share rooms in college with an earnest Welshman on a teacher-training course. Worse still, he soon discovered that in terms of class, Jesus College lay somewhere near the bottom of the University pecking order. Jonas V. Aspinall, who was becoming aware of such things, decided there and then to have as little as possible to do with this shameful institution or its boring undergraduates. (A little hasty in his judgement, he never realised that among his contemporaries at nearby Lincoln College was an undergraduate called David Cornwell who, under the pseudonym John le Carré, became a greater thriller writer in his day than Rider Haggard was in his.)

In spite of this it would be in post-war Oxford that he would discover the first great interest in his life, and it is here that the origins of the Clermont Club began. It is hard to see how this could have happened anywhere but Oxford.

*

There is something so astonishing about Oxford in the early fifties that it is hard to credit that it ever quite existed.

The war had ended, and despite the austerity and the ever-present threat of nuclear annihilation, there was a sense of freedom and euphoria in the air. Some undergraduates of course were very serious. At Somerville there had recently been a chemistry student called Margaret Roberts who thirty-five years later would become prime minister under her married name, Margaret Thatcher. And some of her near contemporaries, like Iris Murdoch, Kingsley Amis and Philip

Larkin had already started writing. But, unlike Cambridge, and most other universities where students were examined at the end of every year, at Oxford this particular treat was saved until Finals, at the conclusion of the three-year course. Thus, for many Oxford undergraduates during this stress-free interlude, lectures could appear irrelevant, work largely optional, and the ancient city was a stately playground where they could make the most of what was left of their adolescence before entering a duller world of grown-ups outside.

'I had not gone to Oxford to study,' the poet Louis MacNeice had written some years earlier. 'That was what boys from grammar schools did.' Jonas V. Aspinall felt the same.

What he did do was to reveal something of the showman in his nature, as he responded to Oxford's precocious cult of youthful celebrity with a sense of urgency to make his name before the golden city's magic spell was broken. Still strongly influenced by Rider Haggard, he would have made a splendid Zulu prince himself, but his provenance and pigmentation were against him. Instead, he tried imitating Oscar Wilde. Even today some of his contemporaries remember Jonas V. Aspinall, strolling down the High in a pink suit and gold waistcoat with an ebony cane and the poems of Wilde's lover, Lord Alfred Douglas, underneath his arm. But he soon realised that imitating Oscar Wilde was not for him. Although he was keeping clear of women, which in the predominantly male university wasn't difficult, he wasn't gay. Nor, as he showed in the one poem he published in a university magazine, was he a poet. Nor, for that matter, would he ever be a wit, like Oxford contemporaries such as Ken Tynan and the still genuinely funny Norman St John Stevas.

While Jonas V. was wondering where his university career was heading, something happened which has a bearing on this story. His stepfather, Colonel Osborne, inherited a baronetcy created in 1629, and overnight the one-time Mrs Aspinall, who had come a long way from the plains of Central India, discovered she was Lady Osborne. Along with the baronetcy went a larger, grander house than the one at Uckfield. This was in the nearby village of Framfield, and once in residence the new Lady Osborne enjoyed the role of lady of the manor.

Her son enjoyed having a titled mother. For somebody like him, Oxford could be uncomfortably snobbish, and until now he had had little real success in scaling the higher reaches of undergraduate society, which in those days could appear forbidding. In this particular world, along with the pleasure of being able to refer to one's mother as 'Lady Osborne', having a baronet for a step-father was not a disadvantage either.

*

No one seems to know exactly when Aspinall first laid hands upon a pack of playing cards. His biographer, Brian Masters, says it occurred one evening while attending a friendly game of poker between some Oxford friends. He became fascinated and after watching long enough to absorb the basic rules, he took a hand himself.

During the next few weeks he continued playing regularly and it soon appeared that he had a genuine affinity with cards and games of chance. This is actually rarer than generally supposed, and casinos make fortunes out of people who imagine they possess it. But it seems that, just as some are born with a knack for languages or writing lyric poetry, so there genuinely exists a small minority with a built-in aptitude for games of chance.

Aspinall was one of them, and the more he played, the more it developed.

His skill came from a combination of qualities. He had unusual powers of concentration and a photographic memory for a run of cards. He possessed stamina, nerves of steel, and a precisely calibrated sense of risk. Once play began his face became inscrutable. At the same time his mere presence, coupled with an instinct for the psychology of the game, intimidated many opponents, and gave him what appeared like an extra-sensory knowledge of their cards and how they would play them.

For him perhaps the most important thing of all was that he truly loved to gamble. As he said later, 'from the first time I settled down to play I felt at home as I never had before.' The excitement invigorated him, the risk challenged him, and he relished the company of gamblers, which came as a relief from those earnest Welshmen back in college.

Later he used to claim that gamblers formed a superior race to passive, tedious humanity, and he rather shocked the journalist Compton Miller by telling him that he 'regarded people who don't gamble as emotional cripples.'

To be able to count himself among the emotionally elect must have been more satisfying than dressing up as Oscar Wilde or studying *Beowulf* or Chaucer, and nobody could doubt his dedication to his chosen field of studies. Soon, most of his waking hours were spent gambling in one way or another.

In his early days his playing was confined to a few old friends for stakes that rarely exceeded ten shillings a game. But as his play improved, he became more ambitious. The stakes rose. Some of his early partners, like John Lawrence, the future Lord Oaksey, became worried and dropped out. 'It was getting too hot for me to handle, and it was obvious that John was heading for the dangerous world of big-time gambling.'

That he reached it faster than he might have done was due to the influence of an undergraduate at Balliol College called Ian Maxwell-Scott. Supposedly the cream of Oxford intellect, Balliol men were not overly given to fraternising with members of humbler foundations such as Jesus College, so the two young men met more or less by chance at one of Oxford's illicit off-course bookmakers. Once they began discussing horses, they realised that they had much in common.

Maxwell-Scott was already something of a university character, a slender, nervous-seeming boy with a very pale face and the appearance of a mad professor. His elderly father, Admiral Maxwell-Scott, had died a few years earlier, leaving his younger son with a trust fund and an indulgent Irish mother. With several serious gamblers already in the family this was a dangerous combination, and while still at school, Ian was already placing bets on horses and running poker sessions in the dormitory. Once at Oxford, he spent his waking hours gambling – and little else.

He was the first addicted gambler Aspinall encountered. Like most habitual gamblers, Ian had grown dependent on the regular stimulus of risk, which he satisfied by pitting himself against the greatest odds, the more impossible the better. Given the chance he would, and often did, gamble on anything with anyone: horses, dogs, baccarat, backgammon, poker, and roulette – he had tried them all. He gambled for the love of it – and for the hell of it. His greatest love was horse racing and for him nothing ever equalled the adrenalin rush of putting every penny he possessed on some rank outsider at the longest odds, and waiting on tenterhooks for the result. If he couldn't bet on horses, he would take a bet on almost anything around – whether the next train from London arrived on time, or whether a crow would settle on the College spire in the next ten minutes. He was known to have taken bets on two drops of rain running down a windowpane.

What particularly impressed Aspinall was the extraordinary equanimity with which Maxwell-Scott bore his losses. Whenever he was totally cleaned out, as he often was, he never seemed downhearted. Quite the contrary. Just as a serious alcoholic returns to the bottle the morning after in order to relieve his hangover, so the confirmed gambler offsets the memory of losing by embarking on another bet. While there's a bet there's hope, and Maxwell-Scott's private antidote to losing was to borrow from any source at hand and go on gambling. A devout Catholic, he even borrowed, so the story goes, from the collection plate during high mass at Brompton Oratory, replaced the cash with a cheque, and put the money on a no-hoper in the 3.30 at Sandown Park. Yet again he lost. What happened to his cheque is not recorded.

Such dedication, and the psychology behind it, fascinated Aspinall, but there were other lessons to be learned from Ian Maxwell-Scott, whose upper-class credentials, though not extravagant, were genuine. The Scott in the name went back in a direct line to his great-great-grandfather, the novelist, Sir Walter. His family was also linked by marriage to a network of catholic aristocrats, headed by a fairly distant cousin, the Duke of Norfolk. Educated, like all the best Catholics, at Ampleforth, he had floated almost as effortlessly into Balliol as Aspinall had into Jesus College.

At this time, the novels of Evelyn Waugh were very much in vogue in Oxford, particularly *Brideshead Revisited*, with its nostalgic atmosphere of impossibly effete young noblemen with impeccable pedigrees facing disaster on the eve of war. Maxwell-Scott could have stepped out of the pages of *Brideshead*, as a kinsman of the doomed grandee, Lord Marchmain.

What fitted Maxwell-Scott so neatly for the part was that, not only did he have the requisite pedigree, but in post-war Oxford he managed to live so completely in the past. As a gun dog knows instinctively how to work the field from centuries of careful breeding, so Maxwell-Scott's entire way of life seemed ruled by an instinctive sense of how a gentleman behaved. It goes without saying that none of his behaviour was remotely tainted with tedious concerns of middle-class morality. In the world of *Brideshead*, unconcern for money was one of the touchstones of authentic aristocracy. Similarly Maxwell-Scott showed his effortless disdain for vulgar wealth by running up large bills for food and wine and good champagne in the college buttery. He ran up yet more bills with his London tailor. He had little hope of paying either – except from a gambling windfall, which he was convinced would come (it would be many years before it did). But he never let this trouble him unduly. If he couldn't pay the tradesmen at the time, someone would pay them in the end. This financial attitude impressed Aspinall and confirmed his gathering distaste for what he believed to be middle-class behaviour, which would continue all his life.

But one should emphasise that Maxwell-Scott was not unintelligent, and along with the curious upper-class behaviour went many other things that Aspinall learned from him during their long and somewhat bumpy time together. Maxwell-Scott was, in fact, a precociously civilised young man. Somehow he had acquired an extraordinary knowledge of food and wine and *recherché* restaurants which was unusual among under-graduates in the early fifties. Aspinall would prove to be a ready learner here as well.

But the true basis of their friendship was always gambling. Maxwell-Scott was rated a good bridge player and a more than adequate poker player, but although as a gambler he wasn't technically outstanding, this never stopped him placing bets with what at times appeared like lunatic abandon. So overwhelming was this passion that he seemed like a throwback to some of the crazily addicted noble gamblers among his eighteenth-century ancestors.

This too caught Aspinall's imagination and he became fascinated by stories of those legendary Whig aristocrats, who had gambled with such apparent recklessness and style. It was a highly romanticised image of a vital, carefree attitude to life embodied in the nonchalance with which great Regency gamblers like Charles James Fox or the Duchess of Devonshire were said to have placed their bets, disdained their winnings and shrugged off their losses. It also involved something of what he had admired in Rider Haggard's Zulu chieftain, Shaka – courage, and a willingness to risk all and damn the consequences.

*

At Oxford in the early fifties there was a thriving group of serious young gamblers among the undergraduates whose days were spent exclusively in games of chance. There was no equivalent in puritan Cambridge, still less in any other English university. With Maxwell-Scott as mentor, Aspinall soon found his way into the most exclusive gambling circle in the city.

This particular group met every day in a now legendary lodging house at 167 Walton Street, kept by a former vaudeville artiste called Maxie. Maxie played, and sometimes overplayed, the role of student landlady as if she were still on stage. The house in Walton Street was, and had been for some time, the perfect place for rich young men to spend their time at Oxford going to the devil. Here even Aspinall soon found himself involved in a far more serious league of gamblers than he was accustomed to.

There was Milo Cripps who would one day inherit his uncle's fortune and title as Lord Passmore; Anthony Blond, the wild and some-times witty son of an heir to Marks & Spencer; Lord 'Civilisation' Clark's son, Alan, who would make his name as a politician and an adulterous diarist; and the son of a wealthy judge, who had already piled up gambling debts of £50,000 at the university. The most exotic character of all was Jocelyn Baines, who lived quite openly at Maxie's with a sultry mistress from Ceylon and who, on leaving university, would write a bestselling life of Joseph Conrad before becoming the first, but not by any means the last, of Aspinall's gambling friends to kill himself. Finally there was Teddy Goldsmith, descendant of generations of Jewish bankers from Frankfurt, who was related to the Rothschilds. Although he was theoretically reading philosophy, he had become addicted to gambling through his friends in Walton Street. 'For a year and a half,' he says, 'we gambled all day. That's all we ever did. There was poker every morning at Walton Street followed by a break for lunch, after which we would generally go racing. There was greyhound racing after supper, followed by the ritual late-night game of yet more poker'.

This was the life for Jonas V. Aspinall. He thoroughly enjoyed himself and although he had no difficulty keeping up with these rich new friends, there was one problem: although most of their betting took the form of IOUs, which might or might not be honoured later, his new friends all had private means or wealthy parents who in the last resort would back their debts. Aspinall had neither.

This meant that he could not afford to lose for long. Gamblers like Maxwell-Scott and those around him could be lured by the addictive thrill of losing, but for Aspinall the real excitement of gambling would always lie in winning, and somehow he ensured that in the end he generally did. As an Oxford friend explains, 'If he lost his shirt one day he'd make absolutely certain that he won himself an even better shirt the next.'

He was very detached and cool about this, and as a gambler he taught himself great self-control. He also revealed an unsuspected vein of puritanism in his make-up. There were two things he saw as real dangers for a serious gambler which he scrupulously avoided: one was women, and he would claim to have preserved his virginity until the age of twenty-five. A still greater threat was alcohol. In the hard-drinking world of Oxford gamblers, he learned that there was a definite advantage for whoever could stay sober longest. As a teetotaller, he always did. Whatever the game and however high the stakes, those pale blue eyes of his had time for nothing but the game in hand and all his concentration went on winning.

Traditionally another function of these formative years at university is to acquire a few close friends who last for life. At Oxford, the relationship between Aspinall and Maxwell-Scott seemed all-important, but later it would change, although Aspinall continued to rely on him and would often help him in the years ahead. But it was at Maxie's house in Walton Street that Aspinall met the man who was destined to become a lifetime ally, a still greater gambler and, after Aspinall himself, the most dominating and important member of the future Clermont Set.

3

A Day at the Races

EARLY IN THE Easter term of 1950 Teddy
Goldsmith found he had a problem in the
shape of his younger brother, Jimmy, who had
arrived in Oxford and was staying at the
Randolph. In itself this did not worry Teddy since
he and his family lived almost permanently in
hotels, but Jimmy should still have been at Eton,
not in Oxford. When Teddy asked him what was
going on, Jimmy told him that his schooldays were
over.

It would always be a moot point whether James
Goldsmith was expelled from Eton, or whether his
decision to have done with formal education
simply coincided with a similar decision by the
school to speed him on his way. What was
undeniable was that he had made a highly original

31

departure from his place of learning and when Teddy saw him he was in unusually good spirits. When Teddy asked where his money was coming from, Jimmy murmured three names: 'Bartisan', 'Your Fancy' and 'Merry Dance'.

When Teddy inquired what he was talking about, he explained that these were the names of three horses which had recently won in three successive races at Lewes in Sussex. He had bet on them to win on what was known as an 'accumulator', where if the first horse wins, the winnings are then placed on the second horse to do the same, and the same again for the third. So great were the odds against anyone choosing three successive winners in this way that for his initial bet of £10, Jimmy had ended up winning £8,000 – in today's inflated currency close to half a million.

Teddy, hiding his surprise, asked his brother what he intended doing with all that money, and Jimmy told him that he planned to stay in Oxford for a few days and would spend his time gambling. As usual Jimmy got his way, and the following evening, Teddy took him round to Maxie's for an evening's poker.

It was a lively session with a lot of money on the

table, mostly in the form of IOUs. Since visitors were not encouraged to participate, Jimmy spent some time watching as the play proceeded. But when the stakes began to rise, he could not resist taking a hand himself, and upped the ante with an even higher bid. Aspinall was banker at the time and, irritated by the way this brash newcomer was taking it for granted that he could bet on credit like the regulars, told him sharply that his bidding had to be in cash – at which the young man produced a wad of fivers, peeled off a hundred pounds, and went on playing.

This made a considerable impression, even on that group of hardened young gamblers, but there was more to come. Jimmy played a practised hand, but by early morning when the game concluded, he was several hundred pounds down. He barely seemed to notice, and settled up from his apparently endless source of fivers without a murmur.

From that night on Jimmy became a welcome visitor at Maxie's, and Aspinall seemed particularly taken with him. He had never seen anyone gambling quite like this before, and despite the difference in their ages – Aspinall was twenty-three and Jimmy just sixteen – that memorable evening was the beginning of what for each of them would be the most important friendship of their lives. It was soon obvious that they had much in common. Clearly both were compulsive gamblers, and both were dominating personalities. What was less obvious was that they were also both outsiders and the young James Goldsmith was the product of a childhood so outlandish that it helps explain the insatiable, driven human being he became.

*

Before they anglicised their name, the Goldsmiths had been Goldschmidts, a family of Jewish moneylenders who had lived for many generations in the Frankfurt ghetto. While the Goldschmidts could never match the phenomenal fortunes stacked up by their Rothschild cousins during the Napoleonic wars, they too became extremely rich as bankers in nineteenth-century Europe. Certainly, when Jimmy's paternal grandfather, Adolph Goldschmidt, grew worried over what was happening in Germany in the 1890s, he was rich enough to be able to emigrate in considerable style to London with his Welsh-born wife, Alice. Having bought himself a

Mayfair mansion, he then purchased two-and-a-half thousand acres at Cavenham near Newmarket, and proceeded to construct the sort of full-blown country seat the Victorians expected of their wealthy families. Like his compatriot and fellow emigrant, Karl Marx, Adolph Goldschmidt had long regarded England as a promised land, and he impressed upon his sons that, although like him, they too had been born in the ghetto, they now had a chance to do what he could not, and take their place amid the English upper classes, to which the family wealth and position entitled them.

His arguments failed to impress his eldest son, Carlo, who became such an addicted gambler that he eventually went off his head and died in a lunatic asylum, convinced that King Leopold of Belgium had cheated him at cards. His second son, Edward, didn't listen to his father either, and became something of a ne'er-do-well. But his youngest son Frank, born in 1878, needed no encouragement to make the most of his adopted country. From his earliest days in London he fitted in perfectly with the accepted pattern of a rich young Englishman growing up in the land of Queen Victoria.

He changed his name from Goldschmidt to Goldsmith, worked hard at a crammer, and after taking a degree at Magdalen College, Oxford, Frank Goldsmith became a thoroughly assimilated, rich young English gentleman. He decided on a political career, worked successfully in local government, and once elected Conservative MP for Newmarket, he seemed assured of a long and happy life as a member of the British Establishment. He was likeable, ambitious, and numbered Winston Churchill, Walter Guinness and Lord Bessborough in the growing circle of his friends. Totally at home in the privileged world that he enjoyed, he had every reason to imagine it would last forever.

In the summer of 1914 when war with Germany became a serious threat, the young MP did his duty, organised the local volunteers and enlisted in his county regiment like any patriotic Englishman. Probably it never crossed his mind that in Frankfurt there were other members of his family every bit as loyal to the Fatherland as he was to Britain. On the eve of war, one of them, Frank's brother-in-law, Ernst von Marx, an official in the German Treasury who was married to Frank's sister Nellie, took it upon himself to send him an open telegram in English, reminding him that if war broke out his loyalties should lie with Germany. The Goldsmiths never quite recovered from that simple telegram.

As caring landlords, they were popular with the locals at Cavenham, but village post offices are not centres of discretion, and once word of the telegram from Germany got round the village, nothing could shield the family from the violent anti-German feeling sweeping Britain. Rioting began and when a group of local 'patriots' tried burning down the Goldsmith mansion, friends and loyal servants had to fight extremely hard to stop them. But for Frank, all his friends' support made little difference. In spite of his position in politics and society, he and his family had been reviled for their nationality. The hurt ran deep. The Britain that he loved had rejected him.

At the time he seems to have disguised his feelings quite effectively and took his place as an officer with his county regiment. When war broke out, he went off loyally to fight the Kaiser, survived the bungled Dardanelles campaign and saw service in the Middle East. But throughout the war, that insult always rankled and in 1918 Frank made it plain that he had no intention of remaining in a country where he felt he wasn't wanted.

By now he was in his early forties and still unmarried, so one can understand how he could cut his losses and begin a new life in another country. But he didn't just leave Britain. He also left behind the self that he had been. In its place he would invent another.

He sold his possessions in England, bade his many friends farewell, resigned his seat in Parliament, and took the train for Paris. There was just one link with the past that he allowed himself. He always liked to be addressed as 'Major Frank'. But once in France, the adaptability the Goldschmidts had acquired from centuries of rootless wandering took over. He had spoken French since childhood, and soon even Major Frank was no more. In his place stood a well-to-do French gentleman known to one and all as 'Monsieur le Majeur'.

After investing unsuccessfully in a chain of cinemas, he used his remaining capital to buy into Hotels Réunis, a management company controlling an ailing group of once grand French hotels, including the Hotel Scribe in Paris, and the Hotel de Paris and the Hotel l'Hermitage in Monte Carlo.

At the time it did not seem a particularly promising investment for him, particularly as he had absolutely no experience of business, still less of running an hotel. But undeterred, the Major took the helm of Hotels Réunis, and slowly set its various hotels in order. As he did so, for the first time in many years, the company started making money, and Major Frank began to realise that these hotels, on which he depended for his living, could also offer him a lifestyle of greater luxury than he had known as a rich young Englishman before the war.

Gradually he, and later, all the members of his family, began to treat these grand hotels as home. Foremost would always be the Scribe in Paris, where the Major kept a permanent apartment, and he was soon getting known for his magic touch at transforming unprofitable hotels into thriving businesses. In time, under his direction, Hotels Réunis would encompass a whole chain of flourishing hotels which he also managed, and in 1932 his company became involved with the Savoy Hotel in London.

M. le Majeur was enjoying a thoroughly enviable lifestyle, but although he had become a respected figure in the world of very grand hotels, he was nowhere near as rich as he appeared to be.

Although he ran Hotels Réunis, he did not actually own any of the hotels he managed, which may be why he put off getting married until he was in his early fifties. This was not from a lack of interest in women, but instead of permitting marriage to distract him from his work, he had indulged in a succession of discreet affairs for many years instead. The last of these was with a famous beauty called Jacqueline Franc, which ended with her death during an operation to make her capable of bearing children.

Following her death the Major became consumed with guilt, making him a sitting target for matchmaking females. It was one of these, a former married friend of Jacqueline's, who sealed the Major's fate by introducing him to her pretty sister just before he left Cannes on the Blue Train bound for Paris.

What happened next sounds more like a kidnap than a courtship, as the twenty-three-year-old Marcelle Mouiller insisted on boarding the train with the middle-aged hotelier, saying she had never seen the inside. Before he could push her off, the train had left the station and they were on their way to Paris. They would stay together until the Major's death twenty-eight years later.

The brashness, resourcefulness and sheer determination with which Marcelle Mouiller caught her Major would reappear in much of the behaviour of her second son, James, as gambler, lover, and businessman in the years ahead. In fact the marriage of Marcelle and the Major was a potent mix of almost total opposites. On the Major's side were generations of inbred Jewish moneylenders, subtle, clever men who carefully considered every move they made, while the Mouillers came from tough French peasant stock from the Auvergne.

Their first child, Teddy, born in 1928, was very much a Goldsmith, with a vein of melancholy that in later life produced a restless, pessimistic Jewish intellectual with a touch of the Old Testament prophet about him, and on the surface little of his father's seemingly effortless business skill. But when Jimmy was born in 1933, the maternal genes took over to produce a maverick Goldsmith full of incessant driving energy, and the passionate aggressive nature of his mother.

It was not until after Teddy's birth that the Major got round to marrying Marcelle, but their devotion for each other was obvious as they happily embarked upon an enviable life together, with the irksome details of everyday life completely taken care of.

Now that he was always living in one or other of his luxury hotels, the Major's life became indistinguishable from that of the richest of his clientele – waited on by the same servants, enjoying the same fine wines, the same elaborate cuisine and always treated by the staff with a deference accorded to none but the grandest of his guests. The Major had a keen awareness of his position. Whenever he departed from one hotel to take up residence in another, the staff would be expected to gather in the foyer and respectfully bid him farewell. By now he had a Rolls, and as his car purred off, with Nelo the liveried chauffeur at the wheel, the head porter would salute exactly as he would have done to departing royalty.

The family spent their summers in the apartment in the Scribe Hotel in Paris and wintered at the Carlton in Monte Carlo. As Europe in the thirties sank into crisis, photographs show the Major and his young wife chatting attentively with Wallis Simpson and the Duke of Windsor on the terrace of the Carlton. A waiter hovers. The royal mistress laughs. Yachts sail on the horizon. The scene repeats itself, with minor variations, with the

Thyssens and the Duke of Westminster. But in all these photographs one thing is noticeable. There is never any sign of the children.

During their months in Monte Carlo, their elderly father, who in many ways was the most doting and indulgent of parents, had arranged for his two young sons to live in the Hermitage Hotel, while he and his wife spent all their time and energies looking after their important guests at the smarter Carlton.

Goldsmith's biographer Ivan Fallon describes the boys enjoying 'a quality of life perhaps only equalled by members of the royal family . . . with waiters, maids, valets, cooks, chauffeurs and door-men only a bell-push away.' But behind the spoiling, young princes live lonely lives. Deeply involved in running their hotels, the Goldsmith parents had little time for them and for much of the day the boys were left to their own devices, looked after by obsequious servants, whom they could treat according to their inclination.

Thus from an early age, Jimmy learned how to deal with staff, impose his will on inferiors, and discovered how to use them to get anything he wanted. This life also accustomed him to take the very best for granted. Nothing else was good enough for him and in years to come he would tend to treat the world like a very grand hotel.

★

Apart from being something of a genius at hotel management, the Major was clearly a charmer – a clever, very busy man who had come to terms with his early disappointment and made a considerable success of life.

But because of their lifestyle he and his wife were shielded from reality almost as much as their two children were. Cocooned in deference, M. le Majeur and his wife were protected from the politics and violence of the world beyond the reception desks of the hotels in which they passed their lives. Whatever was happening outside could be taken care of by the concierge. Within the confines of the hotel, the courtesies of life were carefully observed, and what was happening in Nazi Germany, not to mention the growing anti-Semitism in French society, was barely noticed.

Even when war with Germany was declared, there was no panic, no lowering of standards. Marcelle and the boys were eventually evacuated to the Pyrenees, but the Major took his time to leave Paris and it was only at the last moment that he departed in his Rolls to join his family at the port of Bayonne.

He got there just in time and he and the family had to cram themselves aboard an overcrowded Dutch freighter that carried them to Dover. In London, the family stayed at Claridges while the Major quixotically tried to reenlist in his old regiment. Despite an appeal to his former friend Winston Churchill, the Major, now in his sixties, was unsurprisingly turned down on account of his age. Disappointed he saw little point in remaining in London. He finally found himself another grand hotel to manage, the Royal Victoria Hotel in Nassau in the Bahamas. It was the safest of safe havens for the family to spend the years of war, and for the Major and Marcelle life more or less continued as before. Their old friends the Windsors were staying at Government House and they were soon included in their social circle, together with other members of the idle rich seeing out the war in comfort.

However, life was not so easygoing for the boys when they were packed off to boarding school in Canada. After the sort of life that they were used to it was cold and uncomfortable. Jimmy particularly hated it, and during the Christmas holidays in 1943, unable to get home to his parents, he gave an extraordinary demonstration of independence for an eleven-year-old boy. Without a word to his brother, he ran away from school, caught a train to New York, took a taxi to the Waldorf Astoria, where his father was known to the manager, and checked himself in. With extraordinary self-confidence in one so young, he spent the next day or two entirely on his own discovering New York, and his adventure ended only when the hotel manager contacted the Major who, for once in his life, became furious with his son when he realised he had to make a special journey to New York to collect him and take him back to school.

*

War with Germany all but over, the Goldsmiths returned to England and were soon safely back in Paris, where their apartment at the Hotel Scribe had been kept for them exactly as it was before they went away. The Major, now sixty-seven, resumed his old job at the head of Hotels Réunis.

He was not as affluent now as before the war,

but it was typical of the ambivalence he felt for Britain that just as he still wore English handmade shoes and ate Coopers coarse-cut marmalade, so he sent Jimmy to Millfield and then on to Eton, while sixteen-year-old Teddy was packed off to a crammer where he could be prepared to follow in his father's footsteps to Oxford. It was the Major's ambition for his sons to become the English gentlemen he would never again be himself.

As Jimmy was dyslexic the relaxed atmosphere and special teaching at Millfield suited him. He was even able to continue to gamble and used to bet on horses by postal order. During his time at Millfield he became a confirmed gambler, something he would continue to be for the rest of his life where, according to his admiring biographer Geoffrey Wansell, 'every endeavour was a game which could be won or lost.'

In September 1946, when he was sent to Eton, it was another story. Having always considered himself French he was never happy in this most English of schools. He and his housemaster, Nigel Wykes, never liked each other. Jimmy had no time for sport, was entirely unmusical, and had little interest in education. It was now that he revealed another trait he kept for life. He was a determined hater, and he never quite forgot how Britain had behaved towards his father.

For someone who had grown up in the grandest French hotels, life at Eton must have seemed so uncivilised that as far as possible he ignored it. He was not gregarious. He made few friends and his hatred centred on his housemaster who returned the compliment.

Jimmy had found another source of discontent. He was sexually precocious and, growing up in France, it would have been strange if he had not enjoyed the sexual tolerance which fifty years ago was still one of the more striking differences between the lives of teenage French boys and their English counterparts. It is hard to imagine young James Goldsmith in Paris suffering the frustrations forced on him when back at Eton. At school he seems to have found his principal alleviation in gambling.

At Eton the traditional English upper-class obsession with horse racing meant that there were usually gamblers among the boys and always ways to place a bet. There, one of the masters was the school's unofficial bookmaker. Jimmy was always ready for a game of cards, playing poker or pontoon, and his speed at mental arithmetic proved invaluable for working out the odds for the next days racing.

His taste for gambling started when he was barely six years old. He had been watching an old lady playing on a fruit machine in the Hotel de Paris in Monte Carlo. She had been losing continually and, leaving in disgust, she gave her last franc to Jimmy. He placed the coin in the fruit machine and hit the jackpot. This was something he never forgot. From then on he would always have the confidence to know that if he gambled he could win.

At Eton he had had some impressive wins already, and one thing he did pick up there was his lifelong skill at backgammon and poker. Then came his unheard of win with the accumulator bet at Lewes, which confirmed his status as one of life's predestined winners. When everything in Goldsmith's life became a game of chance, the fabled accumulator bet became a sort of touchstone. Along with his childhood jackpot on the fruit machine, these extraordinary successes against enormous odds confirmed that he was one of the elect to whom the fickle god of gambling sometimes brought salvation, not only from the tedium of Eton, but also from the outside world. All this came as further proof of something else he had learned to take for granted during childhood in those grand hotels – that he was someone special.

When combined with a natural instinct to rebel and rarely to forgive, the result could be forbidding. He showed the tenacious power of his hatred against his housemaster, who became the first of several sacrificial victims who would litter his path to power in the years ahead. Jimmy himself never had, nor would ever have, much use for Beethoven. But knowing that Mr Wykes loved classical music, he bought him a complete set of Beethoven symphonies as a leaving present. On receiving them the master was surprised and touched by Goldsmith's kindness. But after shaking hands, Jimmy asked to have the records back for just a moment, and proceeded to smash them one by one on the floor. He then walked out without a word, leaving the broken shards of the records lying in the study to show just what he thought about his housemaster, about Eton and about England.

★

Once at Oxford, he was in a different world, and

felt instantly at home among the other gamblers in Walton Street.

As a gambler it was clear that he was utterly unlike Maxwell-Scott, addicted to failure and pursuing risk for risk's sake. His attitude was more like Aspinall's. Like him, throughout his life he would be gambling for one all-important purpose – to win, and through winning to attain the freedom and the pleasure he already knew he wanted out of life. During those first few weeks at Oxford he gambled like a maniac until the fivers finally ran out. He also borrowed a friend's exotic girlfriend for a night or two.

When he was finally cleaned out, M. le Majeur was as tolerant as ever, sent him a ticket to Madrid and, trusting he would now come to his senses and follow him into the hotel business, arranged an introduction for him at the Ritz in Madrid to gain some practical experience. Since this consisted primarily of washing dishes, Jimmy did not stick it long. Instead, an Eton friend called Digby Neave joined him in Madrid, and they went on gambling. Finally Marcelle sold a flat that she had bought in Chantilly to pay his debts. Since he had dual nationality in France and Britain, he then opted to do his National Service with the Royal Artillery.

Surprisingly he seems to have enjoyed the discipline. He took a commission, and proved a considerable success as a young officer.

While this was going on, as far as Aspinall and Maxwell-Scott were concerned, Oxford abruptly ended with Finals. It was somehow typical of the examiners to have allowed the examinations to coincide with Ascot week. To be fair to the two undergraduates, they did their best, but for a serious gambler who had to choose between Finals and Ascot week there was no realistic choice.

In the morning both of them turned up in the examination room, but since time was precious, they were wearing grey morning coats and had left their top hats outside. After ten minutes, Maxwell-Scott told the invigilator that he was feeling sick and asked permission to leave the room. Five minutes later, Aspinall complained that he was feeling faint, and did the same. Outside the examination hall, a hired car was already waiting to drive them off to Ascot where they spent a more enjoyable day than they would have done in Oxford. Aspinall won £120 on a horse called Merry Ride. Maxwell-Scott lost every penny he possessed. They returned to Oxford, happy and contented, after a thoroughly enjoyable day at the races.

4

'Daddy I hardly knew you'

NOT EVEN OXFORD, most accommodating of universities, could crown John Aspinall's three years dedicated gambling with a degree in English Literature. When the exam results were published, only the devoted Lady O appeared surprised, but she hid her sadness. To be fair to her son, not even he, despite his optimistic nature, can have expected a degree. But nor was he downhearted. On the contrary, he saw in failure confirmation that there was not the slightest point in trying to change his way of life.

For his mother's sake, Sir George persuaded a friend to consider John for a trainee managership with Burmah Oil, but he failed to attend the interview. He understood his nature and knew exactly what he wanted – to enjoy the life to which he'd grown accustomed, and go on gambling.

He did make one concession, to suggestions that he might become a racing correspondent. Sir William Emsley Carr, proprietor of the *News of the World*, Britain's largest circulation Sunday newspaper, was a near neighbour of the Osbornes. At one stage the two Ladies, Carr and Osborne, having both recently given birth to daughters, could be seen pushing perambulators down the leafy Sussex lanes together. So Lady O had little difficulty asking her neighbour to interview her son, which he duly did at the cavernous head-quarters of the *News of the World* off Fleet Street. Sir William was kind to him, and put him in touch with the paper's current turf adviser. After a few attempts it was obvious that journalism required more dedication than Aspinall was prepared to offer. But he would not forget Sir William. He was a gambling man himself, and they would meet later under very different circumstances.

Throughout his life Aspinall always seemed to have good friends, usually with money, who would come to his assistance when the need arose.

Currently the friend was Maxwell-Scott, or rather Maxwell-Scott's mother, who lovingly produced a thousand pounds from what was left of his inheritance to help her son set up in business. What she didn't know was that the new venture was a bookie's business, and that John Aspinall would be his partner.

Unsurprisingly they failed to make a profit. Racecourse betting has always been something of a closed shop, run by long-established groups with the business more or less sewn up, and methods of their own for discouraging competitors. But Aspinall enjoyed dealing with a little opposition, usually by facing up to it and making his opponents laugh. 'Say what you like about this Aspers geezer, he's a character,' they'd say, and somewhat erratically the business stumbled on with Aspinall shouting out the odds, and his partner, Ian Maxwell-Scott, rarely able to resist a long-odds gamble.

They must have seemed a very odd couple on the racecourse, but what mattered to Aspinall was that news got round among old Oxford friends that he was still very much involved in gambling. Friends like Anthony Blond and Alan Clark thought it fun to come and watch the gentleman bookie in action at Sandown Park or Plumpton. Other friends followed and placed their bets accordingly, as Aspinall guessed they would. Meanwhile in London he and Maxwell-Scott had found themselves cheap bed-sitting rooms in Kensington, similar to those at Maxie's.

Only one thing mattered to Aspinall at this time. Although he had neither money, job, nor prospects, he had no intention of abandoning the smart life or the friendships to which he had grown accustomed in his happy years at Oxford. On the contrary, his proven methods of maintaining his social position through gambling, continued during these first few months in London.

His character was suited to this way of life. He was rarely downcast and never seemed to worry. He loved a challenge and throughout his life he seemed to prosper in adversity. But the truth was that he was living on little but his wits, his considerable vitality, and his mesmerising powers as a raconteur. When the need arose he could also be quite ruthless. One old friend remembers him working for a period as a shill, playing for the house, in a shady poker club in West London, where he learned some unconventional tricks of the trade.

According to his great friend Taki
Theodoracopulos, the Greek gambler, millionaire
and gossip columnist, Aspinall and Maxwell-Scott
devised a system known as 'kiting', which
involved writing a cheque, which was covered by
another cheque dated for the following day. The
financial acrobatics involved in this were tricky,
but 'kiting' enabled them to go on gambling.

*

It was during this apparently aimless period that
something unexpected happened to Aspinall
which changed the context of his life. He had had
little contact with the distant Dr Aspinall since the
breakup of his parents' marriage, and although the
Doctor had religiously continued paying his school
fees while he was at Rugby, nothing had been
forthcoming since. As Dr Aspinall was now living
in retirement in England, and Aspinall himself was
more desperately in need of funds than ever, he felt
that he had nothing to lose by dropping him a line
asking for some financial support. The Doctor
invited him to lunch.

For a father and a long-lost son who had spent
so many years apart, it was a strangely frosty

meeting. When Aspinall got round to making his request, it was met with a curt refusal. And when he ventured to enquire why his father was not prepared to help, Dr Aspinall produced an answer calculated to stop even someone as self-assured as young Aspinall in his tracks.

'Because I'm *not* your father,' said the Doctor.

As cool as ever, Aspinall countered by enquiring who his real father was.

'I think that's something you should ask your mother,' was the answer.

This put a dampener on any further discussion, and lunch concluded sooner than expected. So did their relationship. They never saw each other again.

In later years, several of those who knew Aspinall would comment on an element of coldness in his nature, which must have come in useful now. One would have thought it might have been upsetting for a young man first to lose a father, then to discover he was illegitimate at the same time. But apparently he took both in his stride.

What did concern him was to discover the identity of his real father. Taking Dr Aspinall's advice, he caught the first train down to Sussex and went to see his mother. It was not the easiest of questions for a son to ask a mother, and Lady Osborne's first reaction was of outraged innocence. She burst into tears, she begged her boy to go away. She even slammed the door on him. When he persisted, she said that all that his questions proved was what she had always known – that Dr Aspinall was a bounder and a liar.

Aspinall did his best to humour her, while still insisting that he had to know the truth. She finally gave in as she always did with him. First she recounted what had happened all those years ago beneath the tamarisk tree beside the stream in Naimital. Then she told him all she knew about the young army officer from the Lincolnshires, which wasn't very much. His name was Bruce, but they lost touch when he left India, and she had no idea what had become of him.

Far from ever blaming his mother for his illegitimacy, Aspinall was probably relieved to be freed genetically from all connection with the Doctor, particularly after Lady Osborne told him that he originally hailed from Malta. One can imagine what Aspinall's reaction would have been to the news that he was half Maltese. But now that he knew the truth, he was more determined than ever to discover who his true father really was.

After long and tedious inquiries at the War Office he learned that the young officer from the Lincolnshire Regiment had recently retired and was living on an army pension in London. This must have been a considerable relief to him and, determined to track him down, he traced his flat. When he rang his doorbell, he found himself facing a mirror image of himself twenty-five years older. Both father and son were strangely unemotional at this poignant moment.

'Good Heavens, you must be Polly's boy,' said the father. Aspinall's reply, though not recorded, was presumably equally low-key, and they cautiously shook hands.

He went as far as to invite his freshly discovered offspring in and offer him a drink, but little more was said. Later, relating to Taki what occurred, Aspinall concluded, 'And you know what – he didn't even offer me a fiver.'

Far from being particularly upset by this, it seems to have amused him. Having just escaped from one father, it was probably a relief not to have a demanding relationship thrust upon him by another. But discovering the truth of his conception was also in the nature of a liberating act, for whether by coincidence or not, from this point on he always acted in accordance with his private code of personal behaviour. He had no father he had to please, and no paternal example to live up to. From now on he was sole captain of his fate. From now on, the only obligations he was willing to accept would be those of his own devising.

★

At this point in life, Aspinall came to an important conclusion. Since meeting Dr Aspinall for lunch, he realised that if he was ever going to be rich it would have to be entirely from his own endeavours. He was also coming to the sad conclusion that he was never going to enjoy this happy state from his winnings at gambling.

There is a critical dividing line between those who gamble and those who live off gamblers. The first group forms an almost overwhelming category and until recently Aspinall, like all his friends, had been among them. At Oxford he financed his gambling partly from his winnings and partly from his ex-serviceman's grant of £70 a term. But at last he realised that to make the sort of money he required, his winnings on their own would never be enough. The fortune he had set his heart on would have to come from the gambling of others.

He was more determined than ever now to remain in the smart, upper-class world he had scrambled into in his time at Oxford. In terms of his personality and his friends, this was no problem. As well as being totally accepted as a gambler and a friend, he was becoming something of a social figure. He had never had much difficulty entertaining those around him with his conversation. Now he was learning the much rarer and more useful art of dominating people with his personality. He particularly applied this to members of the upper classes who lived the sort of life he wanted.

What he absolutely had to have in order to remain securely in their company was the one thing he did not possess – money. Most of his friends had private incomes, trust funds, or at least the bankable assurance of a rich inheritance. Aspinall was the penniless son of a penniless major-general.

But there was a solution. As he had learned from Maxwell-Scott, there had always been a flourishing tradition of heavy gambling among the English upper classes. It had grown so fashionable before the war that even an immensely rich aristocrat like Hugh Grosvenor, 2nd Duke of Westminster, could think of little else but losing a substantial portion of his excessive income in French casinos.

According to His Grace's languid entry in *Who's Who*, he 'owned about 300,000 acres in Cheshire and Flintshire, besides an estate in Scotland and 600 acres in London.' What he was far too aristocratic to add, was that those six hundred metropolitan acres formed the heart of Belgravia. The diarist James Lees-Milne gives a memorable picture of the jaded duke 'who would sit up all night at a casino trying to lose the enormous sums of money which his high stakes had brought him in order not to break the bank. Losing was quite a difficult operation, but he managed if he set his mind to it.'

★

Throughout his life, Aspinall was always going to be accused of snobbery. This was not entirely fair. When he chose to he could, and sometimes did, get along with almost anyone, regardless of their class. His problem was that what he wanted was a lifestyle he could find only among his gambling friends from the upper classes. And the only way he could achieve this was with the assistance of *their* money. As his early Oxford gambling partner, Lord Oaksey, said, 'John wasn't entirely a snob, but he had to make his living out of toffs.'

His first serious attempt to do this, though original, was very much in character and formed something of a pattern he returned to all his life.

Not for him the tentative approach. With his old friend Ian Maxwell-Scott, he took a room in the Ritz Hotel and began using it for a series of poker parties. He knew a lot of smart and very rich young men with whom he shared a keen desire to gamble. During his long apprenticeship at Oxford he had learned exactly what they wanted. The rich feel most at ease in the company of the rich and the wealthier the company, at his poker parties in the Ritz, the more profitable would be the play.

He also knew that, although what he was doing was technically illegal, the police would not court trouble by tangling with the smart and obviously influential friends he was planning to invite. Since in those days the Ritz was still a thoroughly old-fashioned hotel, and as he and Maxwell-Scott were clearly gentlemen, the management were even less likely to object.

Nor, as it happened, did the hotel manager dream of questioning their credentials or what they were up to. Their friends were unmistakeably gentlemen as well. Aspinall made sure that the manager heard that some of them were even titled. Thus, against considerably longer odds than even Maxwell-Scott would have accepted, Aspinall's poker parties at the Ritz continued happily for several months.

Champagne was usually on the house; likewise the food, which with Maxwell Scott in charge of the menu could include caviar and lobster, depending on his mood and the availability of funds. Nowhere else in London was gambling so amusing. Nowhere else, provided they were lucky, were gamblers so well fed. Aspinall's guests generally included one or other of the Goldsmith brothers whenever they found themselves in London on a few days holiday from Paris.

At times the play could get a little wild, but no one worried as the guests all knew each other, and the riff-raff were, of course, excluded. For Aspinall, the only real problem was, as ever, boringly financial. And as ever, he and Maxwell-Scott managed to survive entirely on credit. For although he was starting to make money out of poker, there was no way this would ever cover their expenses. He would never settle for a frugal lifestyle and over this period he spent far more than he was earning. In the end, as usual, somebody would have to help him out.

When the management made it clear that the days of poker parties at the Ritz were over, Aspinall found a backer and set up an off-course bookie's business near Oxford Street, called Jonathan and Carlyle.

*

Aspinall picked up a number of invaluable new friends during his gaming parties at the Ritz. Among this growing retinue of accomplices, admirers and fellow gamblers was one who would become particularly close to him during the next few years. Dominick Elwes was a playboy, a womaniser and for a long period enjoyed a reputation as one of the best looking and funniest young men in London. Since he also thought himself something of a gambler, and greatly admired Aspinall, it was inevitable that when the Clermont Club began he would take his place as the third of those five key members of the Clermont Set.

At the beginning what seems to have attracted Aspinall to Elwes was that he had qualities that Aspinall needed for his parties. He was a playboy with a famously shocking reputation. In the debutante jargon of the period he was definitely NSIT – not safe in taxis – which young girls from the upper classes found so irresistible that he could always be relied on to produce a decorative and well-connected girl or two for any of Aspinall's parties. He was also on that ill-defined dividing line between the gentry and the aristocracy. For many years his family had been squires of Billings Hall in Northamptonshire, when an unprece-dented streak of artistic talent suddenly appeared within the family. Dominick's grandfather, Gervase Elwes, after starting out as a diplomat, converted to Catholicism, abandoned diplomacy for a life as a professional singer and ended as a papal knight and chamberlain at the Vatican. A good-looking man, he married Lady Winifrede Feilding, a daughter of the Earl of Denbigh.

Lady Winifrede was what was known as

'artistic', and she encouraged Dominick's father, her son Simon Elwes to attend the Royal College of Art. When the professor in charge, the painter Henry Tonks, expelled him for his weakness as a draughtsman, he went to Paris where he studied under various post-Impressionist painters including Seurat. Once back in England, he followed his father's example by marrying Lord Rennell of Rodd's daughter, Gloria. To support his fashionable wife and growing family, he settled for becoming a successful portrait painter to the Establishment, ending up with a lucrative clientele among the great and good, including royalty.

Dominick was the eldest of Simon Elwes's sons, and at his birth a mischievous fairy godmother granted him those enviable gifts which in stories always lead to trouble. He was charming, handsome and extremely funny, and seemed to have inherited his father's artistic talents. As he grew older it was clear that he had also inherited his father's skill as a storyteller. Simon Elwes was known for the way he could amuse his sitters as he painted them. Like Dominick, he was also something of a womaniser, famous for a long affair with one of his more glamorous sitters, Lady 'Pempe' Aitken. The one gift the fairy godmother failed to give Dominick was something that his father always had – determination.

While at school at Ampleforth, he discovered early on that he could always get his way by making people laugh. Later this talent meant that he was always in demand for parties, holidays and long weekends. Combined with his charm and extraordinary good looks, this meant he usually ended up with the prettiest girl at any party.

Beneath the banter and the charm, he was actually extremely clever, but why waste time on a career, when the world and its women were already there for his enjoyment? Together with his style and social gifts there was much in this attitude, that appealed to the gambling buccaneer, John Aspinall. True, Elwes lacked the dedication and the icy self-control that had already made Aspinall a skilful poker player and a successful gambler himself. But that was not what mattered. In Ian Maxwell-Scott Aspinall already had an ally who more than shared his passion for the gaming tables. But in Elwes he saw something that he knew that he was not – a polished social figure and a womaniser, with a following of glamorous young women and access to important reaches of society which he himself had yet to enter.

5

The Passionate Elopement

IN YEARS TO come members of the Clermont Set would remember 2 June 1953 for two events which coincided on that memorable day. In the morning Elizabeth II was crowned in Westminster Abbey and transformed into the anointed Queen of England. And that same evening saw the start of another transformation. Jimmy Goldsmith met Isabel Patino and began a love affair of such drama and such pathos that it changed him almost overnight from an unknown, spoiled young gambler into a romantic celebrity attracting universal sympathy, envy and and admiration.

At the time the story of these two star-crossed lovers was projected by the media as an extraordinarily touching, real-life popular romance which has never been entirely forgotten. What has never been revealed is that none of this would have happened without the newly-formed alliance of Aspinall and Elwes, who set up the lovers' meeting in the first place. What has also tended to be overlooked is that this touching tale of true love soon became something different – a ruthless battle between the young James Goldsmith and Isabel's father, Don Antenor Patino. At every twist and turn of this bitter conflict, Goldsmith acted with the same gambler's audacity that he would reveal at every subsequent twist and challenge in his life.

★

It all started early that May when Jimmy Goldsmith rang John Aspinall from Paris as he often did, saying he was coming to London for his brother's wedding in three weeks' time. Teddy Goldsmith was doing his military service in England at the time and had been granted a few days' leave in early June to get married. Since this would coincide with the Coronation, Jimmy was hoping to see something of the celebrations while in London, and also hoping that in the evening he and Aspinall could join forces and go out on the town together.

Since finishing his army service, Jimmy had been showing signs of calming down. He was just twenty, and in Teddy's absence had taken over a failing pharmaceutical company Teddy had owned called Dagonal. It didn't sound like Jimmy's sort of thing at all, but soon the company was showing a small profit. With their wayward son suddenly exhibiting more interest in patent medicines than gambling and women, the Goldsmith parents started hoping that his wild days were over.

It was when Aspinall told his new friend Elwes that Jimmy was coming to London, that the idea of the Coronation night party was first mooted. All the biographies of Goldsmith state that this party was organised by the young socialite and gambler Mark Birley, but Birley emphatically insists that not only had he nothing to do with organising it, he wasn't even there.

The idea of the party grew when Elwes told Aspinall that on that particular evening he had been invited out to dinner with a new girlfriend, and that afterwards they would almost certainly want to make a night of it. It might be fun if Aspinall booked a table for that evening in a nightclub. Aspinall and Jimmy could then have dinner there together, and he and his partner would join them later.

But when Aspinall tried to get a booking there were problems. As it was Coronation night London was going to be crammed with partygoers. Top clubs like Les Ambassadeurs and The 400 were already fully booked, and he was lucky to get a table at Al Burnett's less salubrious Stork Room in Swallow Street.

The dinner party to which Elwes had been invited was in fact a very grand affair. It was being given at Claridge's by Don Antenor Patino to celebrate the eighteenth birthday of his daughter, Isabel Patino y Bourbon. Coincidentally, Teddy Goldsmith and his fiancée, Gil, had also been invited. Isabel had known Teddy in Paris, and on hearing that he was now in London on marriage leave, had invited them to the dinner.

Don Antenor had been Bolivian Ambassador in London throughout the war but this alone could not account for the respect to which he had become accustomed. Having inherited a fortune of something in excess of seventy million US dollars, he also happened to be one of the richest human beings in the world. His father Simon Patino, a pure-bred Chola Indian, started life as a Bolivian tin miner. By chance he discovered a disused tinmine that concealed the richest source of the metal in the world, and ended up with an annual income greater than that of his unhappy country.

Upon his father's death Antenor performed the one seriously clever act of his life. Inheriting the massive fortune in its wonderful entirety, he shifted it and himself to Europe, so that when the next revolution came, he and his money were safely in France, where he already had ten villas and an absurd quantity of high-yield property.

Where Antenor was not so clever was in his obsession with creating a social position for himself in keeping with his money. His father had already purchased him a title, which in Spain, as in England, was no great problem for anyone with that much money. Now known as Don Antenor, he had married sixteen-year-old Marie Christina de Bourbon y Bosch la Brus, youngest daughter of the Duke of Durcal who was related to the Spanish royal family. The Duchess of Durcal, as she insisted on calling herself after the marriage, was large, passionate and impossible. Antenor in contrast was small, suspicious and intolerable.

They stayed together just long enough to produce two daughters, Isabella and her older sister, Christina. Having done this, the few occasions when they met were confined to their regular encounters in courts of law in Britain, France and America, where they waged increasingly bitter and expensive lawsuits against each other over the terms of their divorce.

As a family man, one of the few things that seems to have given Don Antenor much pleasure was the recent marriage of Christina to someone called Prince Beauvau-Craon. The fact that Prince Beauvau-Craon worked in a travel agency did not worry Don Antenor, thanks to the two things that the Prince possessed together with his title – a distant family château near Nancy, and a still more distant right to the throne of France. The fact that the château was in serious need of repair didn't trouble Don Antenor any more than the fact that France didn't have a monarch. All that mattered to Don Antenor was to bolster the all-important name of the Patinos.

The Don's snobbery did not stop there. Not content with one son-in-law who was a possible pretender to the throne of France, he set his heart on dark-eyed Isabel marrying, if not an English duke, then certainly the heir to an impressive English title with an equally impressive stately home to match. With her beauty and the promise of finally inheriting half of what was left of the Patino fortune after the Duchess and the lawyers had finished with it, Don Antenor had high hopes of this happening before the year was out.

But little Isabel, with her dusky countenance and flashing eyes, was not called 'Gypsy' by her friends for nothing. She was fun, she was wild and, like her mother, she had a mind of her own. To Don Antenor she may still have appeared like a dutiful daughter, but she was hardly likely to accept his choice of husband if she didn't like him.

As her eighteenth birthday coincided with the Coronation, which they were attending, what better place than what he called 'le Claridge' to launch Isabel into smart London society where she could meet the sort of husband that he had in mind for her? As it turned out Isabel did meet the man she would marry that evening, but not at 'le Claridge', nor in a thousand years would he ever be the sort of husband Don Antenor would have chosen for her.

★

With so much personal happiness invested in his little Isabel, on the night of the party Don Antenor might have paid a little more attention to his other guests, and what they intended doing afterwards. Normally, Don Antenor would have been suspicious of the handsome Elwes, who amused everyone at dinner with his sparkling conversation. Someone had told Don Antenor that Elwes' father was a famous portrait painter. This was not the sort of family connection he was seeking. But the Don was reassured by the fact that this personable young man was accompanied by a glamorous companion, Sarah Chester Beatty (who would marry Lord Brooke a few years later). Nor could the newly-married Teddy Goldsmith be a threat. As for Isabel's partner, young Julian Plowden, son of a distinguished scientist, Don Antenor could tell at a glance that he was not his daughter's type at all.

So after dinner when the younger guests suggested going on to a nightclub, Don Antenor was not particularly concerned. Nor did anyone object when Dominick Elwes explained that, although it would be difficult to find a nightclub on Coronation night, they would have no problem getting into the Stork Room. He knew the owner, the personable Al Burnett, and he and

Sarah had already arranged to go there. This explains how, on the night when Don Antenor Patino believed that his daughter Isabel was in the safe hands of young Julian Plowden, they arrived at the Stork Room to find John Aspinall sitting there with his old friend, Jimmy Goldsmith.

It could have been just the fateful meeting that the subsequent romantic story needed. But Dominick Elwes undoubtedly knew that Jimmy Goldsmith would be dining with Aspinall at the Stork Room that evening. And as far as a gambler like Aspinall was concerned, he would certainly have done all he could to encourage his friend James Goldsmith to chance his luck with one of the richest heiresses in Europe. As for Isabel, in the sheltered world that she was used to, she would never have encountered anyone remotely like this tall, sophisticated young Frenchman.

For Jimmy, from the moment he first held her in his arms on the dance floor at the Stork Room, he must have known that a serious affair with Isabel Patino would be a high risk operation, with the odds stacked heavily against him. But once he embarked upon a gamble, he was never known to quit.

Whatever may have happened in the candle-lit

atmosphere of the Stork Room, Julian Plowden certainly played no part in it. And from that night on, Isabel and Jimmy were inseparable. Since they were both returning almost immediately to France, they had no difficulty meeting back in Paris. As long as Isabel was careful not to arouse the suspicions of her father, she was free to come and go from the great Patino house on the Avenue Foch exactly as she pleased. With Isabel's innocence and Jimmy's experience, it was inevitable that they would soon be lovers. What was more surprising was that at some point rakish Jimmy found himself in love.

Had he not been in love, Jimmy could not have imagined that a father as obsessed as Don Antenor with protecting a great fortune and a hard-won family name was ever going to agree to his daughter marrying what he saw as the penniless son of a Jewish hotelier.

But Don Antenor was being equally unrealistic if he thought that he could dictate to Isabel whom she should fall in love with. And when Jimmy met Don Antenor and formally requested his daughter's hand in marriage, Don Antenor made a still more serious mistake by insulting this formidable young man, whose only crime was to love his daughter. Had the Don been a smarter judge of character, he would have seen at once that this was not somebody to turn into an enemy.

The meeting rapidly became a stormy interview, the gist of which was summed up in the brief exchange which Jimmy possibly invented afterwards. He certainly enjoyed repeating it. Incensed by the sheer impertinence of what Jimmy was suggesting, Don Antenor apparently remarked, 'Mr Goldsmith in my family we do not marry Jews.'

To which Jimmy supposedly replied, 'And in my family, Don Antenor, we are not in the habit of marrying red Indians.'

With which, unsurprisingly, the interview concluded and the first great battle of James Goldsmith's life began.

*

At its climax, the love affair between Jimmy Goldsmith and Isabel Patino was presented in the international press as one of the great romantic stories of the day. As such it has also always been regarded as something quite apart from any subsequent event in Jimmy's life. Writing to Ivan

Fallon many years later, Goldsmith himself described it as 'one of those rare moments, usually brief, in this rather squalid worldly existence, which have beauty and which are pure.'

But the fact is that, from start to tragic finish, what was unquestionably the one great love affair of Goldsmith's life was also conducted like a very high stakes game of poker, with Jimmy anticipating Don Antenor's every move, steadily upping the ante, and finally and furiously outwitting him. As in all the many battles he would fight throughout his life, Jimmy Goldsmith played to win. Had he not done so, his love affair with Isabel Patino would have ended almost before it started.

★

After the stormy interview, the first move was Don Antenor's. Hoping to cool his daughter's ardour, he rapidly packed her off to stay with her sister, now Princess Beauvau-Craon, at her husband's château (now expensively restored with his father-in-law's money). But Isabel had no difficulty informing her lover where she was, and Goldsmith simply caught a tram to Nancy, booked into an hotel, and the lovers went on meeting in secret as before.

At this stage of the affair discretion was still all-important, and throughout the early autumn, although the pair were still in constant contact, Isabel succeeded in lulling Don Antenor's suspicions. So much so that, in late September he decided it was safe to bring his daughter back to Paris, and there she stayed throughout October and November. Don Antenor had appointed two elderly chaperones to guard her, but Isabel was more than capable of giving them the slip, and she and Jimmy continued as before. In mid November she discovered she was pregnant.

For Jimmy this increased the stakes enormously. He was no longer playing a secret game against Don Antenor, simply to meet Isabel and make love to her. Now that she was pregnant, the battle with Don Antenor concerned his right to marry the mother of his unborn child. Somehow Don Antenor got wind of the fact that his daughter and Jimmy were still seeing each other. As yet he didn't know that Isabel was in the early stages of pregnancy, but he knew enough to be enraged at being flouted, and made his next move accordingly. Without warning he arranged for his daughter and one of her chaperones to be flown off immediately on a world tour in his private aircraft. To show that this time he meant business, he also instructed a leading Paris lawyer to start criminal proceedings against Goldsmith for corrupting a minor, on the grounds that in France Isabel was still under the age of consent. To avoid prison, Jimmy had to give a legal undertaking never to see Isabel again.

He naturally refused, but he was in what looked like a hopeless situation. Isabel had vanished, he had little money, and Don Antenor was in deadly earnest and was seriously threatening him with prison. Throughout his life, Goldsmith always had a deep capacity for rage against anybody who opposed him. This could suddenly erupt and engulf his whole existence. It did so now, and instead of throwing in his chips, he angrily continued the contest, sending Don Antenor a message through his lawyer saying that, far from giving any promise not to see his daughter, he would find Isabel wherever she was and marry her.

At this point Isabel managed to get through to him by telephone saying she was being held against her will in an hotel in Casablanca. This left the next move to Jimmy in what was becoming an increasing bitter battle with Don Antenor.

For him to succeed, speed was vital, and using his ownership of Dagonal as security, Jimmy borrowed all he could, and used some of the money to hire an elderly private aircraft in which he was flown overnight from Paris to Morocco. It was a slow plane and a nightmare journey and by the time he finally reached Casablanca, it was only to discover that Don Antenor had once again outplayed him. Somehow he had learned of Jimmy's flight before it started, and long before Jimmy's aircraft touched down, Isabel had been flown back to Paris and secured behind the walls of the house in the Avenue Foch.

Faced with the prospect of defeat, Jimmy kept his head like the experienced gambler he was, and had a stroke of genuine gambler's luck. Back in Paris, not knowing where her lover was, a distraught Isabel had surreptitiously tried ringing his apartment and had got through to his secretary, who gave her his whereabouts and promised to get in touch with him at once. A few minutes later, when Jimmy was telephoned by his secretary, he was able to work out a plan of action. This involved his secretary going to the Patino residence and tricking Isabel's maid with an elaborate excuse into letting her have her mistress's passport. Then Jimmy told Isabel that he was planning to marry her somewhere in Britain, and that his secretary would be booking her on to a Paris-London flight the next morning. Still in Casablanca, Jimmy then called his London lawyer asking him how soon he and Isabel could get married at Gretna Green. Having done this, at this crucial stage of the game, he played his wildest card of all – the press.

Hoping to put pressure on Don Antenor, he had been considering doing this for some time, and had spoken at length about his troubles to Sam White of the London *Evening Standard*, doyen of Paris foreign correspondents, at his customary lunchtime perch at the bar of the Crillon. Later, having second thoughts, Jimmy rang him back, begging him not to run the story after all. But now when White heard rumours of what was going on, like the tough old journalist he was he decided it was just too good a story to waste. So he telephoned his story through to London; but in London someone in the *Evening Standard* office decided it was not worth using and abruptly spiked it.

It was a long time before White forgave his London office for throwing away what would have been his biggest scoop of the year, but in the end he did receive his due reward from Jimmy. Goldsmith genuinely believed that White had ditched the story out of loyalty, and from then on Sam would always be the one journalist in Paris he trusted.

As it turned out the unwillingness of the *Standard* to run the story also did Jimmy an unexpected favour. It left the field open for him to offer an exclusive to a star reporter from what was then the biggest popular newspaper in Britain, the *Daily Mirror*. For as well as talking to Sam White, it transpired that he had also been in contact through an intermediary with one of the *Mirror*'s leading journalists, Noel Whitcomb. Subsequently Goldsmith would play dumb about admitting his involvement with a paper like the *Mirror*, and denied having telephoned Whitcomb from Casablanca. But someone must have contacted him on Jimmy's behalf and made arrangements for what followed.

When Isabel stepped off the plane from Paris at Heathrow next morning, Noel Whitcomb was there to meet her. Moreover, he drove her back to his home, where his wife looked after her as she waited for Jimmy to arrive later in the afternoon. While they waited, Mrs Whitcomb even took

Isabel shopping since she had brought nothing with her and had little more than she stood up in. As well as a toothbrush and a few necessities, Mrs Whitcomb helped her buy a simple skirt and a woollen twin-set in which she was later to be married.

Once Jimmy arrived, he turned the Whitcomb house into his temporary headquarters. First he called his lawyer, who told him that he and Isabel could legally get married in any register office in Scotland, without the consent of either of their parents. All that was needed was fifteen days residence in Scotland before the wedding banns were published, followed by a further week before the marriage could take place.

Jimmy was anxious to keep their whereabouts secret from Don Antenor, knowing that once he discovered this he would do everything he could to stop the marriage. So Whitcomb promised not to publish until this happened. Whitcomb kept his promise, which left Jimmy and Isabel free to continue their elopement incognito.

Sensing victory, Jimmy was starting to enjoy the situation and in spite of the need for secrecy, there was no question of him and a future bride of his furtively slipping up to Scotland on anything as humdrum as an overnight express. Like a gambler on a winning run, he intended that the grand finale of the greatest gamble of his life should be conducted in appropriate style.

He still had what was left of the money he had borrowed from the bank on the security of Dagonal, and remembering how his father always travelled, he hired a chauffeur-driven Rolls and, with Isabel in her new twin-set and the leopard-skin coat in which she had flown from Paris, the lovers headed north. The following evening they reached Edinburgh, where Jimmy's Scottish lawyer and his wife made them welcome in the relative anonymity of their home. And there they lay low for the next fortnight, with Don Antenor, back in Paris, growing more frantic by the hour.

This lovers' idyll in the suburbs of Edinburgh could not last for ever. Officially it ended on 29 December, when their marriage banns were published. But even then, with Whitcomb still sticking to his word, it took two more days for the news to reach Don Antenor in Paris. The moment that it did, the Don flew instantly to Edinburgh. By 2 January he was ensconced in the Caledonian Hotel with an impressive entourage of lawyers, servants and private detectives around him. Even at this late hour he was utterly determined to do everything within his power to stop the marriage.

That same night Noel Whitcomb wrote his story, and next morning the headlines of the *Daily Mirror* told its fourteen million readers the exciting news of the couple's elopement and the desperate bid by Isabel Patino's millionaire father to try to stop it.

The general public, in that relatively unsophisticated age, still warmed to the idea of cruel, rich fathers, impetuous lovers and romantic elopements. And just as the Princess Margaret story two years later was one in which true love between a princess and a commoner was ultimatedly thwarted, so Isabel's status as an heiress, together with her connections with the Spanish royal family, made hers the story of a beautiful girl who was almost a princess, following her heart to be with the man she loved. At the time it was an irresistible fairy tale, and soon all the British and the European press were competing for the story; but thanks to the privileged position of its intrepid correspondent Noel Whitcomb, only in the pages of the *Daily Mirror*, could eager readers follow every detail.

By now there were only three days left before

the couple could marry, and the time had almost come for James Goldsmith to savour victory over Don Antenor at last. What must have been a particular relief to both the lovers was that all that was now required of them was to dodge the detectives and journalists who were combing Scotland for a glimpse of them. Meanwhile, Don Antenor was stuck in Edinburgh, making the worst of an impossible situation. Apart from launching a last-ditch legal action to injunct the marriage, which was rapidly rejected by the courts, there was nothing more that he could do. His misery was palpable and his agony became distinctly comic when his wife, the Duchess, suddenly arrived. Soon they were locked in yet another bitter argument. The hotel was in uproar, Don Antenor was verging on collapse. For the first time in his life, the press began to treat him as joke. This was the moment when James Goldsmith could sit back and finally enjoy his hard-fought victory.

When it came, his marriage to Isabel on 6 January in the Kelso Register Office appeared as the true fulfilment of a wonderful love affair, which in its way, it was. Here the simplest of ceremonies concluded all the dramas and excitements of their forbidden courtship. News of it had seeped out into the little town, and after the ceremony a small crowd of cheering well-wishers was there to greet them. With the need for secrecy over, the couple could now share their happiness with the world's reporters, and back in Edinburgh the new Mr and Mrs Goldsmith faced an enthusiastic press conference like two present day pop stars.

After a night in the bridal suite of a smart hotel, they spent the next day enjoying their new-found role as popular celebrities before taking the overnight sleeper back to London. Just before leaving the hotel, Goldsmith rang Aspinall in London telling him that he and Isabel would be arriving at King's Cross at 4am. As some slight recompense for their part in the affair, he invited him and Elwes to their wedding breakfast at the Ritz.

When their train arrived the crowd of reporters on the platform had been joined by newsreel cameramen with their film-lights glaring. In spite of the early hour, Aspinall and Elwes were also there to greet them and share in their friend's triumph.

When Jimmy and Isabel got back to Paris, they were treated like returning heroes. Then inevitably the excitement faded, and everyday life took over. Don Antenor showed himself a bad loser, and stayed bitter and unforgiving to the end. In contrast, the Goldsmith parents seemed delighted with their new daughter-in-law, and offered the couple an apartment in the Hotel Scribe in which to start their married life. Jimmy and Isabel seemed genuinely happy together (although he now had to work harder than ever to repay the money he had borrowed to finance the whole romantic adventure). With Isabel enjoying a healthy pregnancy, it seemed the perfect ending to their story.

But the gamble Jimmy made that night in the Stork Room wasn't over yet, and the last throw had still to be made by the unseen player who figures in so many famous gambling stories from the past. It was the turn of death to play his hand.

On 12 May 1954, Jimmy left the Hotel Scribe at around nine o'clock to walk to his office at the nearby Place de l'Opéra. Isabel was seven months pregnant now, and he had left her still sleeping peacefully in bed. Then suddenly he felt an inexplicable concern for her and telephoned his mother, asking her to check that Isabel was all right. She found her still asleep, but could not wake her. Thoroughly alarmed she called the doctor, then summoned Jimmy.

By the time he got home Isabel was in a deeper sleep. As the doctor had also been unable to wake her he had called an ambulance. When it arrived, Isabel was rushed across Paris to the American hospital, where the doctors agreed that she had suffered an acute cerebral haemorrhage. The only hope of saving her was immediate surgery to relieve the pressure on the brain. But although the operation was performed early that evening, Isabel remained in a coma. All next day her condition stayed unchanged, with Jimmy desperately hoping that a miracle would happen, but the doctors warned him to expect the worst.

All they could offer now was one faint consolation. With a Caesarean section they could probably save the child – which they duly did, a healthy, five-pound baby girl. Later he would call her Isabel, in memory of her mother who died later that evening. Just before she died there was an emotional reconciliation between Jimmy and his mother-in-law, the Duchess, who had been keeping vigil at the bedside with Don Antenor and the Goldsmith parents. Don Antenor could not make peace with Jimmy, whom he blamed for his daughter's death.

It took Jimmy a long time to recover from his grief. But besides the loss of Isabel, there was a dreadful irony to what had happened. The game that John Aspinall and Dominick Elwes set up for him in the Stork Room on Coronation night had ended with a grim conclusion no one could ever have predicted. Jimmy had won his hard-fought battle with Don Antenor. True the game was over, but in the process, death had robbed him of his wife. Isabel was dead, but her death had also brought him sympathy and affection on a scale that he would never know again.

6

Finding Eldorado

THERE IS A rule which adventurers, social climbers and professional gamblers the world over must remember if they seriously wish to prosper: think big. Make a point of always going for the best. And if you con anyone, go for the rich and famous rather than the poor and the obscure. The rewards are greater, the women prettier, and the resultant lifestyles more enjoyable. Quality, in short, remains the surest policy.

This was one lesson Aspinall had learned in his days at Oxford and had lived by ever since. Why socialise with trainee teachers at Jesus when members of Balliol were richer and more fun? Why live in Earls Court, when he could settle more agreeably in Belgravia?

'Why did you hold your poker parties in the Ritz ?' someone asked him.

'Because I couldn't afford Claridge's,' he answered.

Later, he never stopped insisting that life should be lived as one great cosmic gamble and for someone who seriously believed this, what had just happened to his gambling friend James Goldsmith must have made a most profound impression. For here, if anywhere, was proof positive of everything that Aspinall believed in. It had been hard on little Isabel perhaps, but Jimmy would get over it. Isabel apart, just think of the spin-off from that little flutter he and young Dominick had set up for him when they arranged that he should meet one of the richest heiresses in Europe on Coronation night at the Stork Room.

Through that one gamble Aspinall had made his friend an international celebrity. Of course it could probably have happened only with Jimmy. From that first night at Maxie's, Aspinall had recognized at once that, as a gambler, here was someone special. Jimmy was a plunger. When he gambled, he staked everything he had. Moreover, Jimmy reminded Aspinall of how Napoleon used to ask one question when deciding whether to promote a promising young general to his chosen band of marshals: 'Is he lucky?' Jimmy was.

Gamblers with luck are rare. In Jimmy's case it showed in the way he won against the odds when least expected. Why did that one franc inserted into the fruit machine at Monte Carlo at the age of six produce the instant jackpot which the old lady had been uselessly pursuing all morning? Why did the three horses gallop past the winning post in succession at the Lewes races to win him his accumulator bet at odds of however many million to one? And why had that evening at the Stork Room and the bitter game with Don Antenor that followed, led to that stupendous outcome?

Aspinall didn't know the answer. No one did. Life has its mysteries and luck is one of them.

Just as the two men's shared obsession with gambling formed the basis of their lifelong friendship, so Jimmy would always be the younger prodigy who would sometimes manifest amazing feats of luck against all the odds. 'One day he will rule the world,' Aspinall once remarked about him. In the meantime, Aspinall made sure they kept in touch, for they had something else in common – a shared desire for luxury. 'Luxury is the most addictive substance in the world,' Jimmy used to say. 'Once you've tasted it, nothing else ever tastes so good.' Aspinall agreed.

This craving for luxury meant that, during this period, Goldsmith had to stay in France, and find a way of making money – in large quantities. Unlike most gamblers, he was a realist and he knew that there was only one sure way to recreate the life of privilege and luxury he'd tasted in the grand hotels of his childhood. Not through gambling, that could come later, but through hard work and by using his extremely sharp intelligence.

Although he worked like one possessed, it wasn't easy. With more assurance than experience, he took his fledgling business, Dagonal, into the cut-price pharmaceutical business and began competing with large established companies by selling cheaper products of his own without brand names. The profits, though enough to keep him in a very comfortable lifestyle, were not as spectacular as he hoped, and two years later when he tried to force his way into the British market selling cut-price Cortisone, he nearly came unstuck.

Another of his problems was with baby Isabel. When his mother-in-law, the Duchess, suddenly turned against him and kidnapped her, he felt that he had no alternative but to fight for her through the courts. Being Jimmy Goldsmith, he finally won his case, and got his daughter back and made a home for her with the help of his devoted secretary, Ginette Léry, who had recently become his mistress. None of this was particularly romantic, but it saved on time and money, and despite his international romantic image, the romantic role had never really suited him. Isabel's death had cured him of it for ever.

Henceforth, love was one luxury that he could not afford. It was too distracting and the results could be too harrowing. Sex of course was different. Sex was essential to his being and his somewhat fragile equanimity. In 1959 he had a son by Ginette, whom he proudly named Frank Manes Ernest Henry Benedict Hayum Goldsmith. All this made Ginette very much the centre of his family. But she must have known him well enough to suspect that, like his father, he had always been a womaniser, and that like many Frenchmen of this era he may even have enjoyed regular visits to brothels. In fact, Goldsmith always liked prostitutes. They flattered him and made no demands beyond their fee. It could even be a way of showing off. As his daughter Isabel put it when she was old enough to understand her father, 'Daddy's true ideal had always been a harem.'

One of the few women he worked closely with but did not sleep with, the banker Mme Beaux, once said that at heart he was really a misogynist. Perhaps he was, like many future members of the Clermont Set. But as time would show, this did not render him immune to jealousy, particularly once his precious *amour propre* became involved. But the keystone of his highly convenient personal morality lay in the sacred memory of his tragic first wife Isabel. Since, by definition, no living woman could compete with her, her memory offered him a licence in sexual matters to behave entirely as he pleased.

During this period in Paris, he began to work so hard that for a period he suffered from boils and his hair began falling out. The result was a physical transformation which matched the change in his mentality – from the floppy-haired romantic idol he had been at twenty, into a restless human being, driven, tough and unrelenting, with a head as shorn and hairless as a marine's.

★

Meanwhile his friend Aspinall was similarly preoccupied with making money. In his case this meant trying hard to crack the great elusive secret of how to make a fortune out of other gamblers. After 1955, like Goldsmith with his pharmaceutical companies, he went on trying. He never seemed downhearted or complained and lived his life with remarkable panache. He had always been persistent over anything he really wanted and, like Jimmy Goldsmith, he intended to be seriously rich.

He continued to run Jonathan and Carlyle, the off-course betting business, but there was always something wrong with it. Finally he blamed its failure on its location in an office block in Oxford Street. He maintained that, for some reason, punters didn't feel comfortable in Oxford Street, but the truth was that he didn't enjoy sitting in an office, and would leave Lady O in charge while he went off to earn the rent by playing poker, which was one form of gambling where he could usually count on winning – in one way or another.

Win or lose, he lived his life by two strict rules: never economise and never plead poverty. Even in this straitened period, he did neither, although there were times when he seemed dogged by insuperable small disasters. Friendships soured, tempers were often strained, and cheques bounced like rubber balls around him.

Even the weekend gambling party he arranged for Anthony Blond at the family mansion while his parents were away went horribly awry. It ended with an angry shouting match when Blond's parents unexpectedly turned up when they should still have been safely in New York. Aspinall was blamed, fearful recriminations followed and he ended up badly out of pocket. But whatever happened he was never downcast long and always seemed to come up smiling.

Above all he had the sense to hang in firmly with the upper classes. Not only did a better class of gambler usually have more money to gamble with, but the higher up the social scale, the more likelihood there was of gambling debts being paid. Unpaid cheques are the curse of the gambling classes, and life had already taught him that cheques that bore the name of an ancient family would usually be met next morning when presented at Martin's Bank at the Sloane Street end of King's Road, Chelsea.

He had also hit upon a potentially useful spin-off from his great passion for the turf. As a racecourse regular with a difference, he was soon on friendly terms with most of the rich and influential Newmarket owners, many of whom themselves were great gamblers. These included characters like van Cutsem, the young Duke of Devonshire's trainer, the impressive and eccentric lesbian race-horse breeder Monica Sheriff, and a young Scots millionaire called Bill Stirling. He also got to know two gambling aristocrats with close connections to the turf – John Earl of Derby and finally the thirty-two-year-old Andrew Devonshire himself.

During this period, he relied on Dominick Elwes more than ever for the light touch with women and the sense of fun and glamour he exuded. In those days Elwes possessed something that Aspinall still lacked – sex appeal and success with women – and as a playboy he alone enjoyed the social cachet needed to keep the two of them afloat in the fickle world of smart society. It was not entirely by chance that Elwes was with him on the evening when he stumbled on the lucky break he needed, and the Clermont Club, though still six years away, became a possibility.

*

It was during an afternoon's racing at Fontwell

Park that Aspinall met the Vicar. Although they rarely advertise the fact, it is not unheard of to encounter clergy at the races. But this particular Vicar wasn't what he seemed. Everyone called him 'Vicar', because he looked like one, and spoke like one. Like Aspinall, he was by trade a professional gambler.

Aspinall had sometimes worked for him as a house player when he ran down-at-heel poker parties. It was the Vicar who first showed him how to insert 'the sandwich' – an apparently virginal but actually doctored pack of cards – into a game. It was now several months since Aspinall had seen him, and he had clearly risen in the world. For the first time in his life, he was looking positively prosperous.

When Aspinall congratulated him, the Vicar proudly told him he was now living in a large house in the smartest part of suburban Esher.

'How come, Vicar?' Aspinall inquired.

To start with the Vicar was cagey. 'God moves in a mysterious way,' he answered.

But Aspinall was curious, and in the end the Vicar was unable to resist telling him his secret. He had abandoned poker parties for a more prosperous field of endeavour, running *chemin de fer* parties for respectable people in private houses. Things were going better than expected, and he was suddenly attracting a newer, richer clientele than he had known before. It so happened that he was holding one of his parties for a group of rich businessmen in a flat in Park Lane in a few days' time.

'Just think of that. Park Lane, Aspers!'

Clearly something in the way that Aspinall received this news conveyed an element of doubt which led the Vicar to commit a fatal indiscretion.

'Whereabouts in Park Lane?' Aspinall inquired, and the Vicar told him. Worse still, he invited Aspinall along, together with any rich young friends he knew who might enjoy a flutter.

Neither the Vicar nor Aspinall can have realised the full significance of that invitation. For the Vicar it was like the moment when Red Riding Hood mistook the wicked wolf for her grandmother. For Aspinall it would lead directly to the private gold-mine he was seeking.

He took the Vicar at his word, and made a point of turning up at the party with Dominick Elwes, who also brought along his girlfriend, Sarah Chester-Beatty. The other players that night were mainly rich financiers, and Aspinall's small party brought a touch of youth and glamour to what would otherwise have been a heavy-going evening.

Aspinall and Elwes both lost several hundred pounds that night, far more than either could afford, and Sarah had to rescue them with a cheque of her own. But although the evening might have seemed disastrous, it was nothing of the sort. It opened Aspinall's eyes to two extraordinary chances chemmy offered him. These suddenly appeared so obvious that he could not believe he hadn't spotted them before.

Until the play began he hadn't grasped the operation of something known as the *cagnotte*. The word *cagnotte* is French slang for pot, and on every game a fixed sum, usually twenty per cent of the total stake, is automatically deposited in the pot – in practice a slot cut at one end of the table. This goes to whoever organizes the game, in theory to cover his expenses, and it was this that had financed the Vicar's move to Esher. As well as this, that evening Aspinall also realized how *chemin de fer* could readily appeal to the fashionable and rich young gamblers he was so anxious to impress.

It was clear that the Vicar himself had no earthly hope of introducing this game to the gambling aristocracy. He lacked the personality, the requisite accent, and the *entrée* to society. But sooner or later somebody was bound to latch onto the idea. That very evening, Aspinall made his mind up that he and he alone would seize the chance while it was still on offer.

In mid-fifties Britain there existed an untapped reservoir of uninvested wealth, to which a surprising number of the younger members of the British upper classes had access. All gambling booms require this sort of floating money. In the 1830s William Crockford, a former fishmonger turned gambler, started a fashionable gaming club in St James's, made himself a fortune and, according to the diarist Captain Gronow, within three years 'without exaggeration had won the whole of the ready money in London.' The club that bears his name continues to the present day. In the seventies it was the oil-rich Arabs who had this sort of 'ready money'. In the nineties it was the turn of the Chinese. Today London's top casinos have their sights set firmly on the Russian *nomenklatura*.

Gambling, like most things, goes in fashions. During the thirties, most of the rich gamblers who chose to sacrifice their surplus wealth at the major Continental casinos did so at roulette or baccarat.

Roulette was supposedly the brainchild of the seventeenth century French mathematician and theologian Blaise Pascal, who was so obsessed by chance that, as a devout Christian, he devised a gambler's theorem for believing in the Almighty. Known as Pascal's Wager, it states that however great the odds may be against God's existence, the faintest possibility that He just might exist offers each one of us an immensely long-odds bet that we would be stupid to reject by not believing. Since Pascal was a genius, he also devised the world's first mechanical computer and, as part of an experiment to demonstrate the operation of pure chance, he rather casually invented the roulette wheel. Ever since, Pascal's roulette wheel has offered gamblers the surest way of finding pure untainted chance in the casino – provided the casino owners let it. But for those who finally got bored watching a small white ball bounce across a heavily rotating numbered wheel, they could, and often did, fall back on baccarat.

Played with cards, ritualistically dealt by a highly-trained croupier, baccarat was also regarded as a game of chance. A more sophisticated version of pontoon or *vingt-et-un*, it called for little of the skill required by bridge or poker, but had a glamour and a personal involvement lacking in roulette. It was also more addictive, and produced serious reductions in several legendary fortunes of the thirties. It was by playing baccarat that the Duke of Westminster lost his thousands, and the two legendary gamblers – Gordon Selfridge and André Citroën, their tens of thousands.

Although baccarat is overwhelmingly a game of chance, it can remain susceptible to skill. Nicholas Zographos, an Athenian professor of mathematics, created the legendary Greek Syndicate which dominated the main European casinos between the wars. He once told his biographer Charles Graves that 'the difference between a good and a bad baccarat player is greater than that between a scratch golfer and a player with a handicap of twenty.' He proved his point by playing high-stakes baccarat in accordance with a mathematical formula he had worked out, and died in Paris at the age of seventy eight a multi-millionaire.

Zographos also relied on the fact that at baccarat the bank enjoys a mathematical advantage of 2.7 per cent, and is run by whoever can afford to pay anyone who plays against it. His Greek syndicate, by taking on the bank, could win in the end by having great financial resources to back it. In chemmy the bank moves round the table (hence its name, the Train) and as long as one stayed sober long enough to distinguish hearts from diamonds and clubs from spades, and knew whether to shout suivi or banco, *chemin de fer* probably came closest to the operation of pure chance of any card game in existence.

It was this that made it so addictive. Taki Theodoracopulos (who knew whereof he spoke) compared it to heroin. Or as someone else remarked, 'You don't give up on chemmy. Chemmy finally gives up on you.'

★

One can't begrudge Aspinall his extraordinary success. He had tried long enough and hard enough to make his fortune, and now as he planned his first chemmy party, he showed such flair and love of detail as he made his preparations that he probably deserved to win at last. He began by using much the same technique that he had used at his poker parties at the Ritz. The most important thing was to choose the smartest possible location. So he took over a flat in Mayfair, and hired one of the top Italian croupiers in

London. Between them, he and Elwes arranged the guest list, carefully choosing people who, as well as being serious gamblers, would also turn the party into a memorable evening which everyone would talk about.

Also from his poker parties at the Ritz he knew how all-important it was to provide memorable food and a constant flow of first-class wine. Here, his mother came into her own. Not only was she, like her son, a keen gambler who became known as 'Al Capone with a handbag', but she had exemplary culinary skills and the celebrated game pies she cooked for her son's chemmy parties became famous. Alcohol, essential lubricant of any gambling party, was also plentiful and free – and since Ian Maxwell-Scott was in charge of the wine list, it was probably an improvement on anything served in most of the stately homes in England.

Then came one final touch which showed Aspinall for the true perfectionist he was. He paid a visit to the Leger Gallery in Bond Street, and explained that he intended buying two good pictures for his flat in Brook Street. Had the Vicar tried this they would probably have called the police, but he was so convincing that the gallery let him take a pair of old masters home on approval.

Where he showed true savoir-faire was in the way he selected a small Canaletto and a Panini, two recognizable painters he knew that his aristocratic friends might well expect to find in the home of a gentleman.

His first three chemmy parties were an extraordinary success, both socially and financially, and he must have seen almost immediately the amazing possibilities *chemin de fer* offered him when he realized that he had netted something over £20,000 from the *cagnotte*. This clearly made him careless, and with his fourth game came an unexpected setback. Until then all the guests he invited to his parties were people he knew and trusted, but on this occasion a so-called princess, whom nobody really knew, though several people vouched for her, asked to be invited. He agreed. Then at the last minute, she telephoned to say she was unwell, but was sending along a representative to play on her behalf.

The Princess's representative duly arrived at Brook Street and during the course of the evening ran up losses of £10,000. Instead of stopping there, he asked Aspinall for permission to continue. Since everybody was excited and most of the other players were winning, Aspinall nodded, and the

Princess's friend gave up only when his losses reached £17,000. He wrote out a cheque and trusting the word of the Princess, Aspinall accepted it; backed by this, he paid out winnings to other players. Next morning, the cheque bounced. This practically wiped out all his profits. It was a useful lesson for the future which he would not forget.

One evening a week later, he happened to catch sight of the Princess and her 'representative' dining together at Les Ambassadeurs. Seizing the moment, he marched up to their table and demanded settlement of what they owed him. They tried to brush him off, but an angry argument ensued in which half the restaurant finally joined in, including the film star Robert Mitchum. Fisticuffs in London's smartest nightclub with a film star did no harm to Asper's reputation as a gambling buccaneer. It even made the front pages of next morning's newspapers, but it didn't get him back his money.

7

The Floating Aristocracy

FOR SEVERAL YEARS one subject had been more or less taboo between Goldsmith and Aspinall – sex. This was not for want of trying on the part of Goldsmith, for whom, after gambling and money, sex had always been a favourite topic of conversation. But it seemed that Aspinall genuinely wasn't interested.

'Aspers, I know what you are. You're a secret fornicator,' Jimmy used to say.

'If you say so, Jimmy,' Aspinall would usually reply, and shrug his shoulders. But all of this was just about to change.

It was never explained why Aspinall was sitting on his own one late spring afternoon in 1956 in the tea room at Fortnum & Mason, reading the *Sporting Life* while an afternoon fashion show was in progress. As the models wafted past showing off designer dresses, he looked up and a striking figure modelling a blue silk dress by Hardy Amies caught his eye.

She was tall and beautiful and when the compère introduced her as 'the Spirit of Park Lane', Aspinall felt impelled to find out who she was. After the show he approached her and, before he had even asked her name, he invited her to go racing with him the following afternoon at Sandown Park. Jane Gordon-Hastings, as she turned out to be, agreed to go.

From that afternoon at the races, Aspinall was smitten. For him, the first and foremost test of any human being had always been the ability to gamble and not to count the cost; so he appreciated the way she lost the hundred pounds he gave her to gamble with, then coolly asked him for another hundred.

Despite her beauty and apparent sophistication, Jane was essentially a simple girl at heart. She was also very young and surprisingly naïve. The more he saw her, the more she seemed to be exactly what he needed, and it didn't take long before she was under his somewhat overwhelming spell. When he proposed to her and she accepted, she was just nineteen and he was nearly thirty.

Thanks to that disastrous chemmy party and the behaviour of the Princess's 'representative' he was still all but broke, so the wedding had to be a simple ceremony at Caxton Hall. But Aspinall had no intention of allowing anything as middle class as lack of funds to take the magic from their special day. After a rapid exit from Caxton Hall to dodge a bailiff's man trying to serve him with a writ, they took a taxi to the Connaught, one of the most expensive hotels in London, where he had already booked a suite for their wedding night.

He had also organized a party next day at the hotel for a number of their closest friends. When he booked it, he had no earthly way of paying for it. But, as usual, luck was on his side. One of his wedding presents, a cheque from his rich friend Gerry Albertini, more than paid for the night at the hotel and the party that followed. With the money left over, he decided to take his bride for a honeymoon to Monte Carlo, hoping to recoup his fortunes at the casino. And there, as if by magic, he found salvation in the person of Eddie Gilbert, an effusive American millionaire and fellow gambler.

It was as if Aspinall had conjured him out of the rich, money-laden air of Monte Carlo. While watching him play blackjack, Gilbert became so impressed by Aspinall's success that he asked him to play on his behalf. Aspinall won and went on winning. From then on Eddie Gilbert backed him, helped finance him and put him back in circulation.

While he'd been away, Aspinall had come to realise that he had no need to rent a separate flat in which to organise his chemmy parties. With the social success that he had been enjoying, any number of his rich friends would now be only too delighted to allow their homes to be used, provided he was there to organise them.

But there was a more important reason why Aspinall decided this. According to the archaic gambling laws still in existence in the fifties, established gaming houses and casinos in England were illegal. But gambling in private houses was permitted, provided it did not happen on a regular basis. For the police, continuous gambling on the same premises was taken as evidence of a permanent gaming house.

This meant that he could hold chemmy parties almost anywhere round Mayfair and Belgravia as and when he wanted, so long as they were never at the same place two nights running. Once he was back in London, the era of the so-called 'floating chemmy parties' started, with Aspinall firmly in control of them.

Two of the earliest who lent their homes for the evening were Jean Paul Getty's friend and assistant Claus von Bulow, and the interior designer David Hicks. The gambling set that Aspinall had been building up around himself since Oxford came together with remarkable results. Word of the parties also reached his friends in the wealthy racing set, and before long rich and reckless gamblers like Lord Derby and the young Duke of Devonshire became regular players.

Class and exclusiveness were all-important features of these parties. The bonds that mystically unite the upper classes reassured them all that 'Aspers' was 'one of them', and he seemed to have a knack of making everybody feel important. For some reason, to gamble in the presence of a duke, or even a marquess or an earl, is more exciting than risking one's money with the hoi polloi. It could also create a more carefree attitude, encouraging punters to take risks that otherwise they would never contemplate.

For Aspinall the profits from his parties were sensational. Soon he was making up to £30,000 a night, an awful lot of money in the 1950s.

*

The newly-weds still needed somewhere suitable to live, and having met Lord Cadogan at one of his parties, Aspinall picked up the freehold on a ground floor maisonette in Eaton Place at a knock-down price. Lord Cadogan happened to own most of Chelsea and Belgravia, but after a long run of bad luck at the tables he seemed only too delighted to accept the ready cash that Aspinall could offer.

So married life for the Aspinalls began in the grand style he already took for granted. He was proud of his flat and proud of Jane. She dressed beautifully and extravagantly, and someone who knew her at the time remembers her mentioning that she had poured an entire bottle of Joy, advertised as 'the most expensive scent in the world', into her bath. The Aspinalls employed a couple to look after them and started entertaining lavishly. He bought himself a Rolls Royce, and the rich life started up in earnest.

On its own, gambling is not a convivial activity.

It becomes so only when conducted against a background of partying, sex and gossip, all of which was very much on offer at Aspinall's private chemmy parties. Luckily he loved giving parties, and had a flair for organising them. As a couple, he and his new young wife made perfect hosts, the gambling king of Mayfair with his consort, the Spirit of Park Lane, by his side.

One of the most memorable of his early parties took place at Claus von Bulow's rich mother's spacious flat in Eaton Place. A jazz band was flown over for the night from New Orleans, and the gambling continued until after dawn. Soon 'Aspinall's Floating Chemmy Parties' were getting talked about and written about, and fast becoming something of an institution. With the Vicar safely back in Esher, there was absolutely no competition, and he had the whole rich pasturage of upper class gambling society to himself. Thanks to the operation of the *cagnotte*, a fifth of every pound note gambled at his tables was his.

After his marriage, he appeared more solidly established as a social figure than ever, and began attracting dedicated gamblers who would form the basis of the future Clermont Set.

Dominick Elwes already had a permanent place

among them, thanks chiefly to his wit and his attractiveness to women. Jimmy Goldsmith frequently turned up from Paris, and around this time the fourth founding member of the future Clermont Set made his appearance, another Old Etonian called Mark Birley.

By an odd coincidence his arrival meant that now two key figures in Aspinall's close circle were sons of two of the most successful portrait painters of the day. Birley's father, Sir Oswald Birley, was an older, even more successful portrait painter than Simon Elwes, Dominick's father. Socially the Elweses were grander than the Birleys, but both painters had gained recognition from the Establishment early in their careers. It is fascinating to watch how both these sons were already showing much the same adroitness in the gentle art of navigating through the upper reaches of society, as their fathers.

The paternal influence was important in other ways as well. Dominick Elwes had inherited his father's ready wit and a touch of melancholy, whereas the most important quality Mark Birley seems to have acquired from his father was a lifelong taste for comfort and good living. He still speaks fondly of the luncheon parties which his father regularly gave in his St John's Wood studio for his famous sitters.

In 1954 Mark Birley had married Lady Annabel Vane-Tempest-Stewart, whose grandfather, Charles Stewart Henry, 7th Marquess of Londonderry, had been notorious (like other members of our prewar aristocracy) for his friendship with Goering and Hitler. Although he was one of the very last of the old Irish grandees, the family wealth actually came from the rich coalfields in County Durham. This had immeasurably enriched the Londonderrys in the past, but nationalisation of the coalfields had reduced their income and, like most rich landowners, they were now feeling threats to their traditional position. At the time of Lady Annabel's wedding they were still hanging on to one of the very last great private residences in London, Londonderry House in Park Lane. Six years later, Londonderry House would succumb to the demolition men and the glories of the Park Lane Hilton take its place.

From the start, Annabel's family had disapproved of Birley, who was not considered rich enough or grand enough for their daughter. On leaving Oxford he had been employed in one of the biggest advertising agencies in London,

J. Walter Thompson, where he learned a lot about the art of marketing and selling. This proved invaluable when he acquired the first English franchise for the fashionable Paris-based boutique Hermès. On opening a shop in Jermyn Street he did well, dealing in the whole exclusive range of expensive Hermès ties and silk headscarves.

The couple married, like the Aspinalls, at Caxton Hall. Birley had been a dedicated gambler since his days at Eton and, according to Annabel, he spent the first night of their honeymoon at the tables. In spite, or possibly because of this, their early years of marriage were extremely happy, with the Birleys and their three young children, inhabiting Pelham Cottage, an idyllic country cottage within a stone's throw of South Kensington Underground station.

Another old friend of Aspinall's who now embarked on the lottery of marriage was that carefree gambler Ian Maxwell-Scott and, just as with Mark Birley, the prospective bridegroom encountered opposition from his intended's family. This was understandable as young Susie Clark had a promising career before her at the time, having just become the youngest female barrister in Britain. Her father, Sir Andrew Clark was one of the most eminent criminal lawyers of the day and he objected to her marrying a penniless gambler, even if he was a cousin of the Duke of Norfolk. This was actually somewhat hypocritical on Sir Andrew's part, since he was himself a confirmed gambler all his life. His daughter, who took after him, had her first account with a bookmaker at fourteen, while still at Queen's Gate School for Girls. Since she and Ian were both addicted gamblers, gambling proved the basis of a long and happy marriage. In spite of being responsible for a wife and finally six children, Ian never ceased to be a wild gambler, although occasionally a most successful one. Despite periods of near penury, in old age Susie Maxwell-Scott cheerfully insisted she had never once regretted marrying a gambler. 'Marriage to a gambler like Ian was wonderful' she used to say. 'For me it meant that I was never bored.'

In fact, as long as Aspinall's chemmy parties lasted, Ian was never really short of money either. Aspinall was always generous to his gambling friends and was now becoming seriously rich. No one has calculated quite how much he made, but one conservative estimate quotes the sum of £350,000 in the first year, 1956–7. Today the

Inland Revenue would have wanted a large part of this, but because in those days organised gambling did not legally exist, the tax man was surprised and gratified when Aspinall had the sense to offer him a nominal sum, and permitted him to make his own voluntary tax assessment in future. Amanda Jane, the Aspinall's first child, was born in 1957 followed by a son, Damian, born three years later.

Aspinall never said what took him to Mr Palmer's pet shop in North London early in 1957, still less what made him buy a small capuchin monkey. If you live in Eaton Place and want an unusual pet to amuse your guests, you could do worse than purchase a capuchin monkey. They're small and affectionate and have a zany sense of humour all their own. Livelier than a Pekinese and more affectionate than a Siamese, they take their name from the monk-like hood around their head. This particular monkey was a great success with gambling friends who visited the house. One of them christened him 'Dead Loss'. Thereafter he was always known as 'Deady'.

Deady's popularity turned Aspinall's thoughts to other animals. Like many people with childhood memories of teddy bears, he seems to have regarded bears as friendly creatures, and from Mr Palmer bought a pair of young Himalayan bears. He called them Esau and Ayesha, took them home to Eaton Place and for a while he did his best to make them socialise among his guests. Legend has it that a short-sighted peer once mistook Esau for another member of the House of Lords. But Himalayan bears are not as sociable as they appear, and before long Aspinall reluctantly confined them to a cage that he constructed in the garden.

This did nothing to deter him from trying to make friends with other wild animals. Rather the reverse, and his problems with Esau and Ayesha seem to have convinced him that if only he had bought the two bears young enough and brought them up to have no fear of him, this would have been quite possible.

To prove his point, his next purchase was an orphaned female tiger cub called Tara. There was no question of keeping her in the garden with the bears. She was far too young, and as affectionate and playful as an overgrown kitten. At whatever cost to their sex life, Aspinall insisted that he and Jane had Tara sleeping with them in their bed. As she grew bigger he bought Tara a sturdy dog lead and used to take her for a nightly constitutional round Belgrave Square, very late at night when less adventurous people were in bed.

His animals made humdrum pets like dogs and cats seem middle-class and boring and he soon decided that he actively disliked them. He revealed his true attitude to man's best friend one night, when he took Tara for her usual walk around Belgravia. If anybody noticed, no one objected until one night a lone Alsatian took exception to the young tiger and attacked her. Aspinall's biographer Brian Masters describes what happened next: 'Tara despatched it with one swipe of the paw and a bite in the neck. Then Aspinall quietly dumped the corpse of the rash unthinking brute down someone else's basement stairs.'

Aspinall clearly relished the role of the rich eccentric Englishman keeping a tame tiger cub in Belgravia. But as Tara grew, this clearly could not last for ever, still less would it be possible to keep Esau and Ayesha caged in his back garden. Before long he would have to surrender his animals to a zoo – unless he could find somewhere suitable to house them. With this in mind he started looking for a house with land as close as possible to London. Never one for doing things by halves, he finally discovered a decrepit country mansion in fifty acres of richly-wooded parkland close to Canterbury. It was called Howletts, and by another of those lucky breaks which now seemed to be marking Aspinall's progress, it was said to have cost a mere £5,000, which he supposedly won in an even luckier break one afternoon at the races.

Personally I have my doubts about this, as I bought a small country cottage around that time, in the same neighbourhood, which also cost £5,000. But then, Aspinall specialised in being lucky, and he certainly spent an awful lot more money turning Howletts into the private paradise he wanted. Here at last a number of new exciting roles could flourish as he continued to invent the self that he had set his fertile mind upon creating.

Although the house had had two ungainly Victorian wings added, the core of the building was essentially unchanged. Built in the 1760s, it was a rare example of a genuine Palladian English country house. A huge amount of work was needed for its restoration, but thanks to chemmy, Aspinall could pay for it and was all too anxious to bring Howletts back to its original splendour.

Dominick Elwes was again invaluable. He introduced him to a young unknown architect, Philip Jebb, whom Aspinall took to immediately.

Like Aspinall, Jebb was a perfectionist. He was also something of a genius and saw at once the full potential of the house. To restore it would clearly be a most expensive business, but Aspinall had by now decided that he had to have his stately home. Accordingly Jebb suggested using the most fashionable interior decorator of the day, the legendary John Fowler of Colefax and Fowler, to decorate it for him. Ignoring the expense, Aspinall agreed at once, as he did when Jebb followed this by suggesting Russell Page, the most famous landscape architect in Europe, to restore the garden.

When the Victorian wings were demolished, Jebb found what he expected, the original Palladian façade. The Georgian interior was meticulously restored, with Aspinall insisting that each bedroom have its own bathroom (in those days this was still unusual). By the time the work was finished the house that may have cost £5,000 had had at least a quarter of a million lavished on it.

But Aspinall had another equally important reason for acquiring Howletts. While he was recreating a genuine Palladian mansion in one of the most beautiful parts of England, he was also recreating the role he wanted for himself, that of the eccentric eighteenth century Whig grandee who lived there. 'Establish a character for eccentricity and you can get away with anything,' wrote the philosopher John Stuart Mill, and Aspinall was certainly eccentric. He also realised that here at last was the ideal place that he had dreamed of for his animals. The two bears could have all the space they needed, he could make a home for his tiger Tara, and one day he could find a mate for her so she could rear a family of her own. This would be the beginning of his private zoo, and at Howletts he could live close to the animals who would become as important to him as human beings.

★

Back in London, however, it was business as usual, and he continued building up his coterie of rich, dedicated gamblers. One of them, who became extremely close to him was the young Lord Bingham, heir to the elderly 6th Earl of Lucan. After three years in the Coldstream Guards he was working in the City. Tall and very elegant, he played a faultless game of bridge and on a good day he could beat Aspinall at backgammon. But the game that excited him most was *chemin de fer*. During a weekend gambling at Le Touquet, he had picked up £20,000 in an evening. It was then that he acquired the nickname he would carry for the rest of his days, 'Lucky'.

But Lucky was in a different league from most other gamblers. Firstly he was a genuine aristocrat, descended from a long line of eighteenth-century Irish landowners, and secondly he was already seriously addicted. By becoming a close friend of Aspinall's, he also became the fifth and final member of the group at the centre of the future Clermont Set.

It was around this time that Aspinall showed a growing tendency to direct the lives of those around him. He had always had a dominating personality and when he became a gambling impresario, he brought an element of risk and excitement to the lives of his friends. He liked to tell them that life itself should be a gamble, and towards the end of 1957 he encouraged another close friend to elope with a potential heiress, exactly as he did with Jimmy Goldsmith and Isabel Patino. It was now the turn of Dominick Elwes, who since breaking with Sarah Chester Beatty had enjoyed a number of devoted girlfriends, including nineteen-year-old Tessa Kennedy, whose Yugoslav grandmother had inherited the bulk of the Lloyd Adriatic shipping fortune and was reputedly one of the richest women in Europe.

Just as the Patinos had with Jimmy Goldsmith, so Tessa's parents strongly disapproved of Dominick Elwes, and to forestall trouble her Scottish father had his daughter made a ward of court. Because of this, when Dominick followed Aspinall's advice, and ran away with Tessa intending to get married at Gretna Green, an interim interdict was granted in the court of sessions in Edinburgh preventing them from marrying in Scotland.

But Dominick was no Jimmy Goldsmith, and there and then their attempts at marriage would probably have ended but for Aspinall's encouragement. According to Tessa, it was he who lent them money to fly to Cuba, where they went through a civil marriage ceremony.

Thanks to Aspinall it appeared as if in Cuba their luck had changed. Like the runaway Goldsmiths before them, they found themselves overnight celebrities with much publicity in the international press. Everyone still seemed fascinated by runaway lovers, even the notorious old Mafia godfather,

Meyer Lansky, who was living in exile in Havana, and who took an instant shine to the glamorous young couple, even offering them the bridal suite in his new hotel, the Havana Riviera. As a wedding gift he also gave them a large sum of money to spend in his casino.

Dominick, as usual, was unlucky, but Tessa won so much money that on the spur of the moment they bought themselves a brand new Cadillac. Then their luck truly deserted them. No sooner had they bought the car than Castro's revolution started, and they discovered that their Cuban marriage was of dubious validity. Because of this, they quickly flew to New York, where they went through another marriage ceremony.

But luck had really turned against them now. Once back in England, Dominick was arrested for contempt of court, and spent the next two weeks in Brixton Prison. Eventually the two families were reconciled, but Tessa's family found it hard to trust him, and made sure that any family money was tied up for Tessa and her children. She and Dominick went on to have three sons, Cassian, Damian and Gary, and were divorced eleven years later.

★

As the fifties drew to a close there seemed no reason why the good life of the Aspinalls should not last for ever. They began to entertain at Howletts, and organised lavish safari parties in Kenya, complete with an old white hunter and a private plane. The Birleys, the Elweses and young Lord Bingham were among their guests.

Back at home the chemmy parties continued making ever larger sums of money, with the guest list becoming ever grander. Names like Devonshire, Derby and Cadogan were joined by Suffolk, Bedford, Effingham and Carnarvon, along with many other rich and reckless gamblers like the horse trainer Bernard van Cutsem and the Scottish landowner Colonel Bill Sterling. For a while Sterling became Aspinall's biggest loser when he lost £60,000 to the apparently unbeatable Eddie Gilbert at a chemmy party during Ascot week.

Throughout this time the police had never seriously troubled Aspinall, so long as he kept strictly to his own territory of Mayfair and Belgravia. But the current laws on gambling were out of date and contradictory, and strangely it was

Lady Osborne who made the error which ended her son's monopoly of high-class gambling parties. When she rented a house in Hyde Park Street as a venue for chemmy parties, not only was it on the wrong side of the park, it was also outside what had become Aspinall territory, coming under the jurisdiction of Paddington Police Station. Acting on a tip-off, the police placed the flat under observation. As the law stood, the police had power of search over any premises they suspected of being used for illicit gambling, and soon they pounced, entering unannounced in the middle of a game of chemmy. Jane and Aspinall himself, together with Aspinall's friend and fellow gambler, the handsome Irishman, John Burke, were charged with the old offence of 'keeping a common gambling house'. When the police inspector repeated the charge to Lady Osborne she replied, 'Young man, there was nothing common in this house until you entered it.'

The Aspinalls and their guests, including Lord Mond, then head of ICI, Lord Blakenham, and a van-load of over a dozen élite gamblers, were taken off to Paddington Police Station and charged with engaging in illegal gambling. In all, sixteen guests were bound over for sureties of £25 each 'not to frequent gaming houses, and to be of good behaviour for the next twelve months.' The Aspinalls, Lady Osborne and Burke were finally tried before an Old Bailey jury in March 1958. When they pleaded not guilty, the effect was that the obsolete gambling laws of England were also now on trial.

Throughout what followed it was always rumoured that Aspinall had a police officer on the payroll who kept him informed in advance about the evidence available to the prosecution. Whether he did or not, the hero of the trial was Aspinall's barrister, Gilbert Beyfus, who in his speech before the judge brought out something of the mishmash of ancient gambling laws, some of them dating back to the Tudors, which the accused might or might not have broken. It was such a comic muddle that by the time Beyfus finished, the judge finally dismissed all the charges, and instructed the jury to return verdicts of Not Guilty.

This judgment established a precedent after which it was hard to see any police charge against organised gambling succeeding. The Aspinall case had effectively opened the gates for organised gambling in Britain.

This suited the gamblers, and suited the criminal fraternity even more, who started to organise every conceivable form of gambling in England, from the shady East End *spieler* to open games of chemmy and roulette in the West End. One of the very few gambling entrepreneurs who missed out was Aspinall himself, who soon discovered that his exclusive chemmy parties were no longer exclusive.

Luckily for him he had made so much money in the previous two years, that with rich Eddie Gilbert perfectly prepared to back him, he could afford to sit things out until the government produced its long-awaited law to bring some order to the gambling industry. In 1960, when the legislation made its first appearance in Parliament, it was ironically referred to as 'Aspinall's Law', which in a sense it was. Certainly without him and the Paddington police, the 1960 Gaming Act would not have reached the statute books. By the early sixties, London was on its way to becoming the gambling capital of Europe.

Yet Aspinall himself was out of it. With new gambling clubs legally entitled to provide chemmy and roulette all over London, the golden days of his floating chemmy parties were over. If he hoped to continue making his living out of gambling, he had only one solution. To open up a gambling club himself.

8

The House that Kent Built

NOW THAT HE was abandoning his gaming parties for a fixed establishment, Aspinall was thinking bigger than ever, and ended up with another derelict eighteenth-century house, this time in Berkeley Square.

It was never very clear how Aspinall discovered it. Dominick Elwes related a typically baroque tale of how he once befriended a little old lady in black button boots sitting in a wheelchair who used to live there, and how she had shown him round the all but empty house. Later, following her death, when Aspinall was planning his new gaming club, he said he told him all about it. Perhaps he did. But Elwes was a fabulist, and the truth appears simpler if less romantic. According to John Fowler's assistant, Euan MacLeod, Aspinall had been so impressed by the work Fowler had done for him at Howlett's, that he consulted him over a suitable location for his club. One afternoon Fowler took him for a taxi-ride round London to examine several possibilities.

MacLeod is convinced that Fowler had already made his mind up about the house, which he knew, and the taxi made a beeline straight for Berkeley Square, then stopped outside No. 44 – which solved the problem. Aspinall decided there and then that he had to have it. Since he loved Palladian buildings, and since John Fowler was the greatest expert of the day on eighteenth-century interiors, this seems not unlikely. Nor was it unlikely that Fowler had his eye on restoring and repainting the William Kent interior, which duly happened. And very splendid, if terribly expensive, it all turned out to be.

With all his faults, Aspinall was no cheapskate, particularly where architecture was concerned. As he had shown at Howletts, he had an eye, particularly for the sort of Palladian architecture that had so enhanced the splendour and self-image of the eighteenth-century English aristocracy.

Since buying Howletts he had been increasingly regarding himself as something of a reborn eighteenth-century gambler. To have his own Palladian mansion in the heart of Mayfair would complete the fantasy. In his eyes, this alone made it imperative to find the money for John Fowler's services.

Suddenly, this was not so easy, thanks largely to the FBI, who in 1961 finally caught up with his old friend, fellow gambler and financial backer, Eddie Gilbert, and gaoled him for fraud, taking with him £150,000 of Aspinall's investments. Since Gilbert was another gambler, Aspinall refused to blame him. Nor did he let this setback change his plans.

On the death of the last owner of the house, the freehold had been bought as a long-term investment by a property company belonging to Lord Samuel and Charles Clore. In the meantime, since the house was subject to a preservation order, they were unable to decide upon its future and left it standing empty and unloved. This was no way to treat one of the forgotten gems of eighteenth-century English architecture, created by the genius responsible for the Horse Guards building in Whitehall, much of Kensington Palace, the now demolished Devonshire House in Piccadilly,

Holkham Hall in Norfolk, and much besides.

When he was commissioned to take charge of the building of the new house in Berkeley Square for Lady Belle Finch, the unmarried daughter of rich Lord Winchilsea, William Kent was in his mid-sixties and the greatest architect of his day. He was nearing the end of his long, productive life, and made 44 Berkeley Square a final testament of his magical powers. He died in 1748 within four years of completing it.

Once Aspinall had picked on the house to be his gaming club, he was so excited by it that he let his highly charged imagination carry him away on the subject of its origins. For such a splendid house as this, a royal hand, or to be precise, a more intimate piece of royal anatomy, must have been involved. The mysterious Belle Finch must have had a lover, and a royal one at that. Before long Aspinall was airily assuring everyone that Belle had been the mistress of Frederick, Prince of Wales, the eldest son of George II, and that in return he had bought her the house.

In fact, respectable Belle Finch would have been outraged at the mere suggestion of her having had carnal knowledge of that gross royal personage. She was one of the very few women in London of whom that arch gossip Horace Walpole didn't speak a spiteful word ('A lady of irreproachable morals,' was how he referred to her in his diaries). And the truth was that 'poor Fred', though sex-mad like all the Hanoverians, was far too mean to have paid for as opulent a house as this in return for anything as commonplace as sexual favours. Besides, he required his mistresses to be heavy, blonde and very German, preferably coming from the lush pasturelands bordering the Rhine. Belle Finch, like all the members of her family, was so darkly complexioned that she was often mistaken for Spanish. None of the Prince's biographers makes any mention of her ever having been his mistress.

The truth about the building that became the Clermont, though less romantic, is not uninteresting. Throughout his adult life, William Kent's patron and promoter was the rich connoisseur, Lord Burlington (who gave his name to the Burlington Arcade and his town house in Piccadilly, that survives today as the home of the Royal Academy). It was Burlington who took him as a youth to Italy, and since Lord Burlington's wife was Belle Finch's first cousin, this made William Kent practically a member of the family.

This close family connection almost certainly explains how Kent was called on to design cousin Belle's new house.

What is remarkable about the house is the way it has survived with its interior preserved almost exactly as Kent designed it. On Belle's death, the house was bought by the 1st Earl of Clermont. Born plain William Fortescue in County Louth in Ireland in 1722, and dying eighty-four years later as a belted earl, Clermont based his long successful life as a courtier and politician on total loyalty to whatever government was in power. By winning the Derby for him in 1785, his racehorse, Aimwell, also brought him the title of 'Father of the Turf'.

The only mystery about him is where he found the name Clermont for his earldom. There was nowhere called Clermont in Ireland until he renamed his estate Clermont Park. The only explanation would appear to be that his wife, also a devoted courtier, was a close friend of Queen Marie Antoinette, and since the new earl and his countess often stayed together at the French court in the golden days before the Revolution, he chose his title from the pretty town of Clermont, near Amiens, as a courtly gesture of respect towards their friend, the Queen of France.

Lord Clermont and his wife were childless, and spending so much time in France and Ireland they never felt the need to change Kent's interior into a family home in London. Strangely enough the same applied to Clermont's heir, his nephew William, who on the 1st Earl's death in 1806 became 2nd Earl of Clermont. Since he was also childless, with his death in 1829 the earldom also became extinct, and the house appeared to go to sleep.

It slept for the next century and a half, even while the workmen were demolishing Kent's much grander but less interesting Devonshire House around the corner in Piccadilly, followed by the other eighteenth-century houses on the east and north sides of the Square. It went on sleeping undisturbed throughout the Blitz. Even when Messrs Clore and Samuel bought the freehold, they didn't wake it from its slumbers. It took John Aspinall to do that. It was only when John Fowler had completed his dramatic restoration of the house, that the two old property tycoons finally realised what they owned.

'If I'd known about it, I'd have lived there myself,' muttered Lord Samuel.

'And if I'd known,' answered Charlie Clore, 'I'd

have got the bulldozers in before you noticed and built a block of flats.'

★

Once the house had been restored in all its glory, 44 Berkeley Square gave Aspinall what he needed. Not only did it help to make his fortune, it was also the perfect stage for the new self he had been inventing, and the setting for much of what had been evolving in that extraordinary mind of his. With one final clever touch, he named his club the Clermont. On 12 November 1962, its doors opened with a subscription list of more than seven hundred members.

From that moment it was obvious why he had taken so much trouble with the gilding and the painting and the furniture. What Aspinall had done was considerably more than open one more gambling club among so many others in the city. At 44 Berkeley Square he, together with John Fowler and Philip Jebb, had recreated one of the great surviving aristocratic town houses in central London. And at the Clermont, Aspinall could now act the part of aristocratic host to perfection, treating the members not just as gamblers, but as his guests.

He knew exactly how to coax them, flatter them and make these rich survivors of the English aristocracy feel vicariously at home. Jebb designed a mock Gothic dining room in what used to be Belle Finch's garden. Meanwhile the newly appointed Club Secretary, the gambling gourmet Ian Maxwell-Scott, ensured that the food was better than the glorified public school meals currently on offer at clubs like White's and Brooks's. As an additional incentive, for gamblers and favoured members, food and alcohol were free. Having recently discovered that most opulent of Pomerols, Château Pétrus, Maxwell-Scott, could thus offer them something that only the most discriminating of claret drinkers would have known.

(Incidentally, Ian's appointment as Club Secretary came as something of a godsend to the Maxwell-Scotts who, as devout Catholics, produced six children in fairly swift succession and his salary enabled him to support this growing family. His fortunes as a gambler also took an upswing during this period, a phenomenon which would culminate in an accumulator bet on the horses which surpassed Goldsmith's achievement as a schoolboy at Lewes. Maxwell-Scott reputedly won £38,000 out of which he bought Gants Hill, the country house near Uckfield in Sussex, which would play an all-important part in the final drama of Lord Lucan.)

While Maxwell-Scott was prospering as Club Secretary, Aspinall had also given the hall porter at White's Club twice his previous salary to secure his services. This meant that on entering the Clermont many of the members had the flattering illusion of a welcome from a familiar old retainer who not only knew exactly who they were, but also knew how to address them and could even inquire after members of their families.

Just as with his floating chemmy parties, Aspinall made absolutely sure that at the Clermont it was the aristocracy that set the tone. Now that he had his club, he could feed them and flatter them like no one else in London. Hardly surprisingly they were delighted to be able to indulge in what he never stopped telling them had always been the traditional red-blooded pastime of the aristocracy. After more than a century during which the interfering middle classes had effectively banished organised gambling from England, the descendants of Regency gamblers could once more gamble to their hearts' content in these grandiose surroundings to remind them of a world that they had lost. Such was, at least, the theory.

Throughout his life Aspinall professed a deep and lasting admiration for the famous aristocratic gamblers of the past, particularly Charles James Fox, who was his special hero. But the truth was that the gambling fever which infected the higher reaches of the eighteenth-century aristocracy was the scourge of almost every noble family it touched. No one could regard the last years of the Duke of Devonshire's famous ancestor, Georgiana Devonshire, as anything but totally destroyed by gambling as she staggered on, half blind, her looks decayed, her marriage finished, pursued almost to her coffin by creditors and moneylenders. Nor could Fox's life be seriously regarded as an example which anyone in his right mind would have wished to follow, as the most talented and brilliant politican of his generation lost everything to drink and gambling.

★

The early sixties were a deceptive time. On the face of it, after many years of inexorable decline, the aristocracy was making an erratic comeback, in step with the growing prosperity throughout the country. The rise in rents and property prices was placing unaccustomed sums of money in the pockets of families like the Bedfords, Cadogans, Derbys and Westminsters who were lucky enough to own property in the centres of now thriving cities. The rise of the so-called 'Heritage Industry' meant that grants were available for the nobility to restore what was left of their decaying houses. Some even managed to offload financial responsibility for them to the National Trust while remaining as tenants in perpetuity.

But behind the appearance of some sort of upper-class revival, what was actually occurring was that the long decline of the aristocracy had all but run its course, and with the social changes building up throughout the sixties, the aristocracy was being superseded by the new plutocracy.

More people were becoming vastly richer in that prosperous decade as City institutions like the Stock Exchange and Lloyd's opened their boardrooms, previously reserved for members of the upper classes, to the sharper offspring of the growing meritocracy. Takeover bids and property speculation offered others golden opportunities for acquiring immoderate amounts of wealth. A new class of money men was now appearing and the richer they became, the more many of them attempted to assume the habits and pretensions of the vanishing ancient aristocracy.

In the early forties George Orwell wrote that 'No country under the sun is more obsessed by class than England'. It still was. Class obsession had been endemic among the English for so long, that it wouldn't go away, and in the sixties, the very rich appeared, if anything, more class-obsessed than ever as they infiltrated, one by one, the former strongholds of the old nobility.

It was against this shifting background that the Clermont flourished. In fact, it was by no means the exclusively aristocratic institution Aspinall implied when he told his biographer of all those dukes and baronets and viscounts among its members. When I enquired, nobody appeared to know the precise composition of the Clermont's original membership. Strongly encouraged by Aspinall and friends from the days of the floating chemmy parties, a lot of people with impressive titles certainly had signed up, but as the novelty wore off, the Club's regular clientele settled down to a mixture of genuine aristocrats together with a lot of suitably enriched members of the aspiring

English gentry and a hefty intake of rich, high-rolling gamblers of every race – including Greek shipping magnates, Italian industrialists, French playboys and American and Australian billionaires.

To begin with there was a choice of games including backgammon, roulette and baccarat. But as Aspinall knew quite well, the most important game, which he encouraged them to play, was still *chemin de fer*. The *cagnotte* had actually been banned under the 1960 gaming legislation, and replaced by a table charge levied on every game, which rose in accordance with the money on the table. Although Aspinall now didn't earn so much on a single game, what with higher stakes, an ever widening rich clientele and continuous play throughout the year, the gambling was more lucrative than ever.

From the earliest days of his chemmy parties Aspinall had relied on 'house players', usually friends he could trust whom he paid to gamble on his behalf. They were needed early in the evening when extra partners were required to get the gambling started. Theoretically once the games got going and more regular players joined in, the house player would tactfully retire.

As Aspinall used them, house players could be of great importance in creating the right atmosphere among the other players. And as he soon discovered, the curious camaraderie among Old Etonians formed a sort of bond between rich upper-class gamblers. This was one area where the famous old school tie was still effective.

When organising his earliest chemmy parties, Aspinall called his house players 'the Blues' and gamblers who came to play were known as 'the Reds'. Club membership, together with use of the restaurant, was free for the Blues, and they were paid a basic salary of £10 a week.

From the start the Clermont prospered, thanks largely to Aspinall himself and to the club's growing reputation among the richest gamblers in Europe. From the start he also knew the value of celebrities. That mean old misery Jean Paul Getty was so very rich that he could hardly be excluded even though he was far too stingy for a flutter. Kerry Packer was admitted because he was a billionaire and an addicted gambler. John Betjeman was also made a member because his mistress was the daughter of a duke, and Aspinall enjoyed his poetry. Betjeman didn't gamble, but was so enamoured of Kent's architecture that one of his particular treats was to wander into No. 44, gaze at the staircase and the ceiling of the great gambling room, then enjoy lunch and a bottle of Château Pétrus in Philip Jebb's mock-Gothic dining room.

Aspinall had highly original ideas of how to get publicity for the club and keep its members happy. The most memorable of these were his Clermont parties which were quite unlike any other parties ever held in London.

He devised them with the help of his brother-in-law, Anthony Little, an illustrator and designer who had married his half-sister, Jennifer. Aspinall was devoted to him and between the two of them they produced a series of exotic parties loosely based on some of the most way-out themes in history. These included Mithridates, King of Pontus, who went into battle with the Romans with his troops dressed in coloured tunics and ostrich feathers, and Guatemoc, the last emperor of the Aztecs. Although no expense was spared in order to amuse his guests, Aspinall told Little that he really gave the parties to amuse himself.

The most gregarious of men, Aspinall needed large numbers of devoted friends around him. For each of them the Clermont seemed to offer something very special. For Dominick Elwes, who loved his children but couldn't cope with marriage, it was the perfect haven to escape to. He was easily bored with his own company, and had little money of his own. He had never really been a gambler, and although he tried to write a book with his friend, Nick Luard, it hadn't worked. Ominously entitled *Refer to Drawer*, it told the story of a high-class con man who bore a disturbing resemblance to himself. The only funny thing about the book was that it wasn't funny. His humour was in the spoken, not the written word, his wit the wit of instant repartee. As a talker and a storyteller he was unsurpassed, but he was dangerously dependent on an appreciative audience and came to regard members of the Clermont as one big extended family. He hated being called the club's court jester, but that effectively is what he was. He talked for his supper – and for anything else that he required. For many years, both at the Clermont and at Annabel's, he was never presented with a bill. Women sought his company, not only because he was good-looking but also because he made them laugh. Rich members knew that with Dominick among the guests, a dinner party or a weekend house party would be certain to succeed. Behind the socialising, however, he longed to be a successful portrait painter like his father. But successful portrait painting calls for dedication, and Dominick was dedicated only to the Clermont.

The Clermont soon became a home from home for young Lord Bingham too. He had recently married Veronica Duncan, whose younger sister Christina had married his friend Bill Shand Kydd the year before. Lucky, who wanted an heir but whose interest in gambling left him little time for the pursuit of women, seems to have settled for his old friend's pretty sister-in-law as something of an easy option. In time they had three children and a house in Belgravia, but life in the bosom of a growing family was not for Lucky. Having abandoned his career in merchant banking he needed something more to occupy his days and provide at least a fleeting semblance of an occupation.

In 1973, when his father died and he became the 7th Earl of Lucan, Lucky did not weep. In recent years father and son had rarely seen eye to eye. The Lucans had always been regarded as a touch eccentric and in 1945 the 6th Earl, having commanded the Coldstream Guards in North Africa, abruptly joined the Labour Party, ending up as Leader of the Opposition in the House of Lords. At this point Lady Lucan also gamely joined the Labour Party. It was perhaps predictable for the son of such unpredictable parents to turn into an out-and-out reactionary. Once he was 7th Earl of Lucan, it was almost inevitable that Lucky also became the Club's particular adornment.

For the third member of the group, James Goldsmith, the opening of the Clermont proved of more practical value. Having discovered that in Britain there was a treasure trove of asset-rich old family businesses, he began buying many of them to create his groceries company called Cavenham Foods, after the old Goldsmith family estate in Suffolk. As well as introducing him to figures in the world of politics and high finance, at this crucial point in his rapidly developing career the Clermont also offered him the entrée to fashionable society at an elevated level. Given time, it would even seem as if the Clermont would provide him with a springboard from which he could bounce back into that place in British society and politics, which Frank Goldsmith lost when he abandoned England.

The last of the original members of the Clermont Set for whom the club would prove a dramatically mixed blessing, was that most elegant and stylish of gamblers, the tall ex-advertising man Mark Birley. Since marrying Lady Annabel he had been enjoying an idyllic married life with her and their three children in their cottage in Kensington, but selling Hermès scarves in Jermyn Street had its limitations for somebody as smart as him, and he was clearly in need of a challenge. This was something that John Aspinall, James Goldsmith and the Clermont would provide him with, in one way or another, in the years ahead.

9

Annabel's and After

ACCORDING TO the poet Philip Larkin, 'Sexual intercourse began in nineteen sixty-three.' So did the Beatles and the Rolling Stones. And so did Annabel's, the nightclub which opened in the basement underneath the Clermont, becoming what one writer claimed to be 'without risk of exaggeration, the best known and most chic discothèque in the world.' Perhaps it was.

Whereas Aspinall was very much aware of what he had been up to on opening the Clermont, the beginnings of Annabel's were somewhat casual. Aspinall had originally thought of starting a nightclub at the Clermont himself. Instead there came the untimely disappearance of his friendly fraudster, Eddie Gilbert, with £150,000 of his capital, and that was that. Aspinall did not repine, and once the Clermont opened he had too much on his mind to think about opening a nightclub.

Mark Birley says that his original reaction to the idea was to think in terms of little more than a piano bar in the basement. His ideas began to change only when he discussed them with Philip Jebb. When Jebb had had a chance to look at the Clermont cellars he became excited, as a good architect would be, by the Gothic vaulting William Kent created. According to Birley, Jebb remarked, apropos of nothing in particular, that the space would make a perfect nightclub. Coming from Jebb this was stranger than it sounds, since at the time he had never set foot in a nightclub in his life. But it started Birley thinking. To begin with he continued to be wary, and it was only when his brain had started picking up on some of the things he'd learned in his days in advertising that he realised that Jebb was on to something.

According to Rosser Reeves of the Ted Bates Agency, the great panjandrum of fifties and sixties advertising, in order to succeed, any product has to have what he called a USP, a 'Unique Selling Proposition'. Birley worked out a USP for a night-club with a bluntness worthy of Reeves himself. 'It must smell,' he said, 'of exclusivity and sex.'

He had originally thought of calling it Black's. Had he done so, it is unlikely that the club would still be doing the thriving business that it does today. Instead, he decided to simply name it after his wife. Although he may have acted for sentimental reasons, this was yet another stroke of clever marketing. For in her person, Lady Annabel Birley embodied the two prerequisites he wanted for his club. Not only was she very classy, she was also very sexy. Which in those days, when most English ladies with authentic titles looked like Ottoline Morrell or Vita Sackville-West, was most refreshing.

*

To begin with, Birley had trouble finding financial backers. One benefit of this was that, as a result, the original membership consisted largely of Birley's friends, or friends of friends, and he did his best to continue this in future. Whether it was actually true or just a story leaked cleverly to the press, Peter O'Toole was apparently refused entry on the opening night, which seems to have created the impression that getting into Annabel's was only slightly easier than becoming a Fellow of

All Souls or a member of the Académie Français.

As far as the actual club was concerned, Birley was very smart at putting down the sort of social markers that proclaimed Annabel's as upper-class territory. The décor, for instance, made no concessions to anything as vulgar as the modern world. Instead he and Jebb created something reminiscent of the so-called 'English Country House Style' which John Fowler supposedly invented and used throughout the Clermont. Entering Annabel's gave one the feeling that one was going to a party in an old house in the country. This echoed Birley's own childhood at Charleston Manor, his parents' dreamlike country house hidden in the South Downs near Alfriston in Sussex. The food at Annabel's was very much in character, and he created something of a Birley style of cookery, also apparently built round childhood memories of the lunches Sir Oswald served his grander sitters in his studio. Birley didn't want to imitate the food upstairs in the dining room of the Clermont, where, as somebody remarked, 'if you weren't careful you could find yourself up to your elbows in foie gras.' There was no foie gras at Annabel's, just very good quality, glorified nursery food of the sort supposedly relished by unregenerate members of the English upper classes: Dover sole, crab cakes, and a very special shepherd's pie. The most sophisticated dish on the menu was the then fashionable steak Diane.

Whatever exclusivity the food at Annabel's possessed came from its being very good, and terribly expensive. Someone once complained to Birley that he could eat cheaper at the Ritz. 'Go there then,' was his reply. The one speciality almost everyone remembers was the bitter chocolate ice cream, produced by the chef according to his own recipe which included a very secret ingredient. Ice cream aficionados swore it was the best in London.

Something else fondly remembered by girls who frequented Annabel's was the ladies' cloak-room. This was partly thanks to the cloakroom attendant, the legendary Mabel, who looked after them and was always there to listen to their troubles. There was also the giant bottle of *Calèche* scent on the dressing table. (In fact Birley was not being as extravagant as members might have thought, since *Calèche* was made by Hermès, where he still had friends, and free bottles of their bestselling eau de toilette were part of a regular promotion.) So rich was the clientele and so lavish the tips that the man who parked the cars is supposed to have sent his son to Harrow on the proceeds.

An important feature of Annabel's was that it was actually a disco. In itself, this was not particularly original. London's first disco was opened in Soho eight years before by the young Terence Stamp in the days before he was an actor, but the way the two turntables at Annabel's maintained the flow of the latest hits meant that from the start, though classy to the point of stuffiness in terms of image, the club was definitely hip as far as music was concerned.

Birley's keen awareness of the sexual revolution going on around him was even more important. Larkin was right; for all sorts of reasons, 1963 really was the year when the great tectonic plates of sex abruptly shifted, and girls who previously didn't suddenly *did*. At Annabel's, with its low lighting and couples umbilically entwined in near pitch darkness on the tiny dance floor, no one could be recognised and almost anything could happen. 'It was,' as one old Annabel's warrior recalls, 'a great smooch scene.' But a smooch scene laced with luxury: 'Glamorous young couples in evening dress would come on after the theatre or a ball, and there was always a celebrity or two, or at any rate someone who looked like a celebrity.'

And of course, there were the Birleys. Mark was a very tall, good-looking figure gliding through the shadows, ensuring that the Irish linen napkins, the Danish silver and the Venetian glass were all in place. Close by was Lady Annabel, siren, enchantress and resident muse of the Clermont Set. Between them they managed to convey the feeling that this happened to be their home, and that you were very fortunate indeed to be there.

In his determination to preserve the club's exclusivity, Birley insisted that every male guest wore a dark suit and a tie. He permitted absolutely no exceptions, and over the years the list of Annabel's distinguished *refusés* included Eric Clapton, George Harrison and Prince Andrew (who arrived in jeans). Politely but firmly the doorman turned all of them away.

As far as Aspinall was concerned, the most important thing about Annabel's was the cast iron circular staircase tucked away behind the ladies' cloakroom, linking it with the Club upstairs. For Aspinall the two-way traffic that passed up and down that staircase was all-important, for without it the Clermont would have continued much as it began, as an exclusive, predominantly male gambling club. But thanks to Annabel's staircase, the house that Kent built more than two centuries before, for a lady-in-waiting to a Hanoverian princess, became a social landmark of the sixties. As Aspinall's biographer Brian Masters put it, 'Thus the two symbols of extravagant sixties hedonism, the Clermont Club and Annabel's, existed one above the other, in the same building.'

★

While this was happening, Aspinall himself remained something of a puzzle. Although he admired the aristocracy, identified with them and flattered them quite shamelessly, he was also fleecing them outrageously. Most of that multitude of dukes and marquesses and earls he laid claim to on the original membership list came and went, but enough of them remained to give the Clermont the *éclat* it needed. Those he particularly valued were among the richest of his noble regulars like Edward John Stanley, 18th Earl of Derby, Andrew Cavendish, 11th Duke of Devonshire, and the rich, apparently carefree Henry Vyner who, although without a title, was the grandson of the Duke of

Richmond and Gordon and had inherited several thousand Yorkshire acres, a stately home at Studley Royal and the ruins of Fountains Abbey, which Cyril Connolly once called one of the architectural wonders of England. Addicted gamblers to a man, this noble trio not only regularly lost great sums of money at the Clermont, they also helped to set the tone the Clermont needed to attract still richer, though humbler punters.

As befitted members of our old nobility, they were also very stylish losers. Vyner had somehow managed to acquire the habit of treating his losses as a joke. It was a joke that his wife Margaret failed to share. Because of this she couldn't bear the sight of Aspinall. 'The truth was that, being rather middle class myself, I regarded losing large amounts of money at anything as infantile as *chemin de fer* as quite ridiculous. I'm afraid that, for me, the Clermont seemed the height of pretentious decadence.'

Whether it was decadent or not, Vyner continued to enjoy the thrill of going there and losing. He finally lost both Studley Royal and Fountains Abbey, though not in fact from gaming at the Clermont, but from speculating in overseas investments.

Lord Derby was an altogether sadder case. In

spite of owning much of Liverpool, he was not overburdened with intelligence. He was congenitally restless, and married to a flighty wife who dogged his life with drama and disaster. In 1952 while dining at Knowsley, the impressive family seat in Lancashire, one of the footmen started shooting at her with a Schmeiser machine gun, wounding her in the neck. He continued firing, killing two footmen before being overpowered and ending up in a mental hospital.

Being childless, Derby saw himself as 'the last of a once triumphant line' which boasted a previous Lord Derby who was twice prime minister, and who turned down the offer of the crown of Greece on the grounds that 'he preferred to be King of Lancashire.' Bored, lonely and king of nowhere in particular, Derby chose to drown his disappointments in drink and gambling. Once seated in his favourite chair at the Clermont with a whisky and soda at his elbow, he became oblivious of his worries and his losses. One memorable evening he was playing chemmy opposite the head of Fiat, Gianni Agnelli, at £5,000 a game. At one point Derby was winning by £150,000, and Agnelli attempted to cry off, but His Lordship would not hear of it. Agnelli reluctantly agreed and the game continued. Derby bancoed for £20,000. Agnelli suivied and won. Derby bancoed for £40,000, and the same thing happened. Finally, when Derby had lost £200,000 Agnelli thought the time had come to call it a day. This time Derby reluctantly agreed. As he staggered away from the table, he turned to someone standing by. 'Who was that Spanish looking chap I was playing with?' he asked. 'Only a foreigner would have cut and run like that, just as I was about to beat him.'

Unlike Lord Derby, Andrew Devonshire was far from unintelligent. Nor was he particularly unhappy. Years later, looking back on his gambling years at the Clermont, he dismissed them as 'a not uninteresting part of my retarded adolescence.' He claimed to be the one addicted gambler in his family since Duchess Georgiana. Like her, he said, he never won.

As with Henry Vyner, far from letting this deter him he said that 'for me the real attraction of gambling was the terrible excitement of losing. This gave every evening an extraordinary atmosphere of risk. I found this utterly addictive, and before long I was unable to resist entering that smoke-filled room at the Clermont night after night and playing until two or three in the morning. By then whatever luck I may have had had totally run out.'

The Duke said he always found something 'icey' about Aspinall himself. 'This was partly because he didn't drink or smoke or show much interest in women. He told me once that women interfered with his concentration. And he was of course a gambler with a difference.' He always won!

While he did not think that Aspinall was 'actually immoral', he always considered him 'amoral' because he never stopped people playing when he knew quite well that they could not afford it. He emphasised that this did not apply to the way Aspinall had treated him. 'In fact I could afford to lose, and though it's true I lost a lot, and my losses were often most embarrassing, they were never actually disastrous.'

What finally made him stop gambling was the fear that he was losing control through his growing addiction to *chemin de fer*. 'I remember waking up one morning, after yet another night of heavy losses at the Clermont. I felt like death, and said to myself, "What you are doing is utterly ridiculous, and a total waste of life." And there and then, as I lay in bed, I decided I would stop. I have never entered a casino since.'

Another famous Clermont loser was the rakish, six-times married Earl of Kimberley who lost at the marriage stakes almost as regularly as he lost at chemmy. But supposedly the biggest loser of them all was neither English nor an aristocrat, but reputedly the richest man in Australia, the billionaire media tycoon Kerry Packer. The truth was that, provided any gambler was rich enough, Aspinall would always waive his theoretical insistence on confining membership of the Clermont to the upper classes.

One member who was considerably lower down the social and financial pecking order than Kerry Packer was the celebrated 'Fred the Spread', an eccentric, rich industrialist whose patent way of making sure of winning something every time was to place a thousand-pound chip on every number on the roulette wheel.

Another rich non-aristocratic gambler was Aspinall's one-time Sussex neighbour, the press tycoon and proprietor of the *News of the World*, Sir William Emsley Carr, who offered Aspinall his first job after leaving Oxford. To show his gratitude, Aspinall gave him the privilege of joining the ranks of the Clermont's most embattled losers. In all other respects a very shrewd businessman, Sir

William's wits deserted him the moment he set foot inside the Clermont. Knowing his weakness, some of the club servants plied him with alcohol, and since the house players were all Old Etonians he was unshakeably convinced that at the Clermont he was gambling with gentlemen.

The journalist David Leitch, on an assignment for the *Sunday Times*, described how one night he saw Sir William at the Clermont on a horrifying losing streak. 'Fuelled by brandy from the liveried footman at his elbow, he kept losing until dawn when they bore him off like a dying bull. It was a vignette from Genet, not Fleming; primitive cruelty in fancy dress.' By that time in the early morning Sir William was playing both with and against the house players some of whose task it was to keep the game going until he was totally cleaned out. Since he was an honourable man, before collapsing into the cab waiting at the door he insisted on settling the night's debt with the club cashier.

Aspinall felt not the slightest obligation towards anyone he knew who was gambling above his means. He once showed his attitude towards irresponsible young gamblers in his sharp reply to a member of the Cabinet, who wrote to him complaining of the way he had let his young son go on gambling, ending up with such enormous losses that he had had to pay them. In his reply Aspinall could never be accused of pandering to influential politicians: 'I would happily separate any drunken youth from the maximum he could handle, or his family could handle, without the slightest compunction,' he answered.

One rather sees his point. Whatever his age, anyone who started gambling at a club like the Clermont must have known the score.

★

With the Clermont now the most profitable casino in Europe, Aspinall had finally attained the life and luxury that he had always wanted. He enjoyed a glittering social life; he was among the gamblers he loved; he was charming and much admired; he was rich and powerful. But behind the deference and the endless sociability he lived with, there was something strange about the man. When he started the Suicide Stakes at the Clermont, it seemed quite harmless and something of a joke. What could be more amusing, if a touch macabre, than his idea of each week posting up, the odds on whichever member of the club was most likely to kill himself? Like much in his life, Aspinall probably picked up the idea during his schoolboy reading, in this instance from a sinister little tale by Robert Louis Stevenson entitled 'The Suicide Club' in which members of the club enlivened their existence by drawing lots for one of them to kill himself.

There seemed little chance of this happening at the Clermont. As Aspinall knew quite well, addicted gamblers like the racing correspondent, portly Charles Benson, or Ian Maxwell-Scott, rarely kill themselves as long as there remains the faintest chance of one more gamble. But what in retrospect appears a little creepy are some of the other names that appeared on the Suicide Stakes. There was Robin Douglas-Home, for instance, playboy, unsuccessful gambler, talented musician and friend of the famous. After his uncle Alec Douglas-Home succeeded Harold 'Supermac' Macmillan as Prime Minister in 1963, Aspinall was more than delighted to appoint the new prime minister's nephew resident pianist at the Clermont at £50 a week. He found his place on the Suicide Stakes when he started losing most of his week's earnings at chemmy. Aspinall was later infuriated when Robin sold a photograph he had taken of him with one of his tigers in his swimming pool at Howletts to the *Daily Express*. Overreacting to what he felt to be a gross betrayal of trust, he sacked his pianist on the spot. Although this happened at a bad time for Douglas-Home, when his self esteem was particularly low, there was no suggestion that Aspinall's act might have driven him to suicide, but the fact remains that later, in a fit of deep depression, he did kill himself.

Someone else who had also been on the list killed himself not long afterwards. This was Mark Watney, a member of the famous brewing family, and an old member of the Clermont. There had been rumours of a friendship between him and Jane Aspinall.

In the end Aspinall grew tired of the game, and the Suicide Stakes were discontinued. But not before he had included another of his closest friends, Dominick Elwes, on the list.

*

With money and success, Aspinall grew in self-confidence, and increasingly appeared to dominate the lives of the members of the Clermont Set. He seemed to enjoy their increasing dependence on him, especially when they were old friends. Some of them like the Birleys and the Binghams he would take abroad on lavish holidays, cruises around the Greek islands and on a memorable safari to the Serengeti.

After John Bingham became the 7th Earl of Lucan on his father's death in 1964, Aspinall described him as 'my sixth or seventh best friend', he wasn't quite sure which. But his 'number one best friend' would always be James Goldsmith. When he was living in Paris, not a day would pass without them having a lengthy telephone conversation, and every summer one of them would rent a seaside villa in Italy or the south of France where they and their families could share their holidays.

The Birleys had always been key members of the set, but once Annabel's began to rival the Clermont as a social draw, the relationship between Birley and Aspinall began to change, and an angry row suddenly blew up between them. Legend has it that it concerned the wine cellar which was shared between Annabel's and the Clermont. When I recently asked Mark Birley about it, he answered that it happened so long ago that he honestly could not remember what it had really been about. 'What is true is that for many years we didn't talk to one another. And what is also true is that I'm very glad it happened. If nothing else, it stopped me gambling. If I'd gone on playing chemmy it would have ruined me in the end, as it ruins everybody if they let it.'

The truth was that, however trivial its origins, the disagreement opened up a fault line in the two men's friendship which, as fault lines do, widened with the years. With time it led to the eventual breakup of the Clermont Set itself. On the surface it was a very gentlemanly feud which seemed at first to have no effect at all on the other members of the set or on Annabel. She and her three children continued to enjoy Aspinall's magnetic company, and despite the coolness between him and Mark, they continued to visit Howletts.

Around this time Annabel had become friendly with the former model Sally Croker Poole, the Indian Army colonel's pretty daughter who, by marrying a younger brother of the Marquess of Bute, had become Lady James Crichton-Stuart. The marriage hadn't lasted, and she was now having an affair with Jimmy Goldsmith. While this was going on, Annabel recalls that she still barely knew Goldsmith, except as a friend of

Aspinall's: 'When I met him I tended to regard him as very much a café society figure, and really not my type at all.'

During the early sixties, Jimmy Goldsmith's restless life was increasingly attracting him to England. He had always held joint Anglo-French nationality, and was determined to enjoy the very best of what both countries could offer. In Paris he was still living with his former secretary, Ginette Léry, the mother of his first son, Manes. Ginette was also looking after Jimmy's Patino daughter, Isabel. For all the high romance and drama which surrounded her conception, Isabel had not grown up an easy child. Although Jimmy had been granted custody of her, her mother's unforgiving family had kept in close contact with her and influenced her strongly. Ginette's role as her father's mistress and her unofficial stepmother was predictably uneasy. Jimmy found Isabel a problem.

One can understand his relief when he escaped to London. With the opening of the Clermont, it must have been like old times playing backgammon with his best friend Aspinall. He usually won and before long Jimmy was acknowledged as the champion backgammon player in the Clermont. In England there were also exciting business possibilities. As well as Cavenham Foods, he embarked upon another venture with his Iraqi friend Selim Zilkha, setting up a chain of shops which they called Mothercare.

But as always with Jimmy, women were all-important, so when he met the tall, cool, dark-haired Sally Crichton-Stuart he could not resist her. Ginette was the embodiment of the loyal secretary and faithful Gallic wife and mother (even if she wasn't Jimmy's wife) and Jimmy had grown very fond of her, but when he calmly informed her of his plan to set up a separate home in London with Sally Crichton-Stuart, she was in no position to do much about it.

To sweeten the pill he assured Ginette that this would in no way change her position as mother of his son, stepmother to his daughter and precious hub of his domestic life in France. She knew quite well that, like all Frenchmen who could get away with it, a number of the Goldsmith men had always kept a mistress in addition to the mothers of their children. This must have come as wintry consolation for Ginette, but being French herself, and having no alternative, she accepted.

To begin with so did Sally Crichton-Stuart. Like most of those who met him, she found

Goldsmith charming and attentive, but being English she was not as understanding as Ginette over her future or her status in society. She made Jimmy understand that if their relationship was to continue he would have to promise her what he had always managed to avoid promising Ginette: marriage.

This presented him with a serious dilemma. As a Goldsmith, he believed firmly in the tribal and dynastic obligations of his family. How could he offer Sally what he had denied the mother of his son and centre of his family in France? He decided he would level with both women and propose a deal that neither could refuse. To Ginette he would offer instant marriage in order to legitimise his son Manes and reassure her of the social and financial security of her position. Having done this he would then divorce her as soon as legally possible, leaving her with all her rights as a married woman. Then he would marry Sally. As reasonable women, how could either of them possibly refuse?

Neither did. But just for once, fate stymied him. No sooner was he married to Ginette than she discovered she was pregnant with his second daughter, Alix. Back in London when Jimmy broke the news to Sally, she failed to see the funny

(*Above left*) One of the richest human beings in the world and the young James Goldsmith's enraged opponent in the battle for his daughter Isabel's hand in marriage – Don Antenor Patino.

(*Above right*) Goldsmith also had to cope with the Don's estranged wife, Christina Palatino, Duchess of Durcal.

(*Right*) To the victor the spoils. James Goldsmith, having won his legal battle with Antenor Patino, celebrates with Isabel on the eve of their wedding.

(*Left*) The most romantic widower in Europe. After the death of his wife Isabel, James Goldsmith embarks on the role of single parent to their daughter, also called Isabel in memory of her mother.

(*Below left*) Artist's son marries marquess's daughter. Despite opposition from her family, Mark Birley, son of society portrait painter Sir Oswald Birley, marries Lady Annabel Vane-Tempest-Stewart at Caxton Hall.

(*Below*) Another key figure in the future Clermont Set also embarks on marriage; the lunatic gambler and passionate gourmet, Ian Maxwell-Scott and his bride Susie, daughter of eminent barrister, Sir Andrew Clark.

(*Right*) High priest of gamblers, showman of genius and close friend of tigers and gorillas – John Aspinall, at the time his Mayfair gambling parties were introducing the British upper classes to the dangerous pleasures of *chemin de fer* and making him a fortune.

(*Left*) Repeat performance. Like his friend James Goldsmith five years before, another future member of the Clermont Set, playboy Dominick Elwes elopes with his heiress, the nineteen year-old Tessa Kennedy. To avoid a court order taken out by Tessa's father forbidding them to wed in England, and partially financed by Aspinall, the couple headed for Havana on the eve of Castro's Cuban revolution. Here they try their fortune on a Cuban fruit machine before fleeing to New York where they married.

(*Above*) 'One of the forgotten gems of eighteenth century architecture', which became the centre of London high-life in the 1960s, No. 44 Berkeley Square, home to John Aspinall's Clermont Club and Mark Birley's famous night-club, 'Annabel's', in the basement below.

FACING PAGE

(*Above*) The King of gamblers gambles with his life. John Aspinall romps with his tigers at his private zoo near Canterbury.

(*Below*) The start of all the trouble. John Richard Bingham, having recently become the 7th Earl of Lucan, marries the former Veronica Duncam in November 1963.

After attempting unsuccessfully to 'breed' with his second wife, the former Belinda (Min) Musker whom he married (*above*) in 1966, Aspinall was more successful with his third wife, formerly Lady Sarah (Sally) Curzon (*right*). He described her as 'a perfect example of the primate female, ready to serve the dominant male and make his life agreeable'.

(*Left*) 'Our love's no secret anymore.' James Goldsmith and Annabel Birley brave the cameras during a break from his high court action against 'Private Eye' magazine in July 1976.

(*Below*) 'Something new after all those debutantes and heiresses.' Dominick Elwes with glamorous BBC TV researcher Helen Jay at the start of their relationship in 1971.

(*Above left*) Dominick Elwes with John Aspinall aboard James Goldsmith's yacht during a cruise around the Greek islands during the summer of 1972.

(*Above right*) Briefly free from the world of the Clermont Club, Dominick Elwes on horseback in Spain.

(*Right*) Lady Lucan, shortly after the murder of Sandra Rivett, her children's nanny.

(*Above*) Paterfamilias. James Goldsmith
with his wife Annabel and their three children,
Jemima, Zac and Ben.
(*Below*) Goldsmith's last stand.
James Goldsmith campaigning for his
Referendum Party in the 1997 Election
shortly before his death.
(*Right*) In spite of everything still the best of
friends. Mark Birley and ex-wife, Lady
Annabel Goldsmith at the fortieth anniversary
of 'Annabel's', the nightclub they founded.

side of it. She left Jimmy and went off with another very charming Clermont gambler, Philip Martyn.

Later still, on a skiing holiday at Chamonix, she met a dark-haired young man who became particularly interested in her. As chance would have it, he was the thirty-two-year-old, good-looking, vastly rich, highly sophisticated and still unmarried Aga Khan. When he asked her to marry him, she accepted. Tough on Jimmy, but a good career move, Sally.

This time it was Jimmy who failed to see the humour of the situation, and he took Sally's behaviour badly. For the first and probably the last time in his life, he had been dumped by a woman, instead of vice versa, and was beside himself with rage, as he tended to become when thwarted. As usual it was his best friend, Aspinall who tried to put things right, just as he had helped him six years earlier, when he set up that fateful date for him with Isabel Patino.

As Aspinall knew quite well, Annabel Birley was becoming bored and restless at around this time. She didn't like being left at home each evening while Mark went off to Annabel's leaving her with nothing much to do except organise the children and get them off to school next morning.

According to Goldsmith's biographer Ivan Fallon, it was Aspinall, once again taking charge of his friend's life, who encouraged the affair that duly followed between Annabel and Jimmy. Legend has it that he did this by betting Jimmy several hundred pounds that he could not become the lover of the notoriously virtuous Annabel. Whether Aspinall did this out of genuine concern for his old friend Jimmy, or to score off his new enemy Mark, my readers must decide.

With time, Birley appeared to effectively condone his wife's affair. He refused to condemn or divorce her, and continued to maintain their family in Pelham Cottage, thus keeping Annabel's friendship and affection. This supremely rational arrangement did not suit Jimmy. Soon it was he who was eaten up with jealousy while the husband appeared positively grateful that the wife he loved was refusing to go off with her lover. As for Annabel, like the pragmatist she was she soon adapted to her role as Goldsmith's lover, Birley's wife, and the still devoted mother of their three children.

When Mark finally moved out almost seven years later, it was only to a house in the adjoining street, whose garden conveniently backed on to the garden of Pelham Cottage so that the children could come and go between their parents exactly as they pleased.

The contrast could hardly be greater with Aspinall's behaviour to his wife when, in 1966, he discovered Jane had been to bed with one of the men who looked after the chimpanzees at Howletts.

Aspinall was congenitally hard on women. Disloyalty in any relationship had always been for him the greatest sin. Once he decided to divorce Jane, that was that. Under the sadistic divorce laws still in force in the sixties, a woman's adultery was treated as a crime against the legal property of the husband, and an erring wife, legally 'the guilty party', had no rights against him. Like many women in a similar situation, had Jane had money of her own she would have been able, at the court's discretion, to fight for custody of her children. Since Jane possessed no money, Aspinall was able to exclude her from her children's lives. Once the marriage ended, as far as the children were concerned she was cast firmly into outer darkness. Later Damian bitterly complained of how he always felt the lack of his mother throughout his life, and despite the determined way his father fought Jane for custody of his son, once the fight was over his father had little time for him. 'I always felt that he loved his gorillas more than me,' he said.

The frosty side of Aspinall's nature was very much in evidence in the way that, having ended one marriage, he started on another barely six months later. His new wife, Belinda 'Min' Musker, was a pretty, charming and adaptable brunette, who was also very good with animals. It was lucky that she was present on the day the most grotesque event of all befell the Birleys and the Aspinalls.

10

'Tyger, Tyger . . .'

ONE MORNING IN the spring of 1970, Annabel Birley took her three children off on a secret excursion. They were in the middle of the Easter holidays and were beginning to get bored in London. Annabel knew quite well that, because of the rift between Aspinall and her husband, Mark might not approve of her taking their children to Howletts, but the children had been nagging her to take them just the same, and when she spoke to Aspinall on the telephone, he had joined them in their pleas. So on Easter Monday, having told Mark that she was taking the children to the New Forest for the day, they took the train to Littlebourne instead. The next stop after Canterbury, Littlebourne is the nearest station to Howletts. When they arrived,

Min Aspinall was there to meet them with her car.

At Howletts the Aspinall family was out in force to greet them, Aspinall himself, his two children Amanda and Damian and his two half-brothers, James and Peter Osborne. The children were excited to see each other again, and they could hardly wait to visit Aspinall's famous gorilla colony. Housed in a huge cage, which he called his *gorillarium*, they were the largest breeding colony of gorillas in captivity. As usual when Aspinall was present, the whole party entered the cage, and while the children played with the baby gorillas, he made a great performance of wrestling with the big silverback male. Aspinall and the gorilla were old friends, and there was apparently no danger for anyone. In spite of this, Robin Birley didn't seem particularly at ease with what was going on.

After seeing the gorillas, Aspinall was anxious to take them all to see one of his young female tigers called Zorra. Annabel was not so keen on this and wouldn't let her daughter, India Jane, enter the cage with the other children. Like Damian and Amanda, Rupert was used to the animals, but Robin was nervous, though Aspinall persuaded him to approach the tiger and stroke her. Aspinall turned his back for just one moment. In that split second the tiger, sensing Robin's fear, rose on her hind legs, put her front paws on his shoulders and pushed him to the ground. Snarling, she took the boy's head in her mouth.

Seeing what was happening, Aspinall leapt towards the tiger, and with a show of strength somehow prised her jaws apart. By doing this he undoubtedly saved Robin's life. Min Aspinall, meanwhile, was tugging at the tiger's tail trying to prevent its rear claws tearing at the boy's body. Somehow, between the two of them they made the tiger drop her prey.

Rigid with fear at the nightmare taking place before her eyes, Annabel watched as James Osborne rushed forward and picked up her son, who was still conscious. Rupert and India Jane were terrified and screaming. As James carried Robin out of the cage to safety, Annabel could see that the lower left-hand side of his face was crushed past recognition, his mouth had disappeared and part of his jaw was hanging by a thread.

Min drove Annabel and Robin at top speed to the casualty department at Canterbury Hospital. That night the surgeons performed a nine-hour operation on the twelve-year-old boy to save his life. It was only now, as Annabel waited, not knowing if her son would live or die, that the magnitude of what had happened hit her, and she collapsed. She felt totally responsible. Later that night she had to face her husband who had rushed down from London when he heard the news. As she wrote later, 'He was very, very angry.'

Her misery apart, it still seems unbelievable that two supposedly responsible adults like Aspinall, and Annabel herself could ever have permitted young children to enter a cage with a grown tiger in the first place. Were they mad? Were they wildly irresponsible? Or were they simply very stupid?

In fact all three of them had reasons of their own. The story behind these reasons is extraordinary, and the outcome of that day is more extraordinary still. But first, the story.

It starts in 1957 when Aspinall first discovered Mr Palmer's pet shop in Regent's Park Road and bought Dead Loss the capuchin monkey. There in that stuffy little shop, amid the smell of birdseed, catshit and the musk of monkeys, Aspinall was not just purchasing a pet. He may have been unaware of it, but he was also acquiring an alternative existence. From that day on he started living two separate lives.

One was the life of the most successful gambler in London, who would soon be revelling in the luxury and the acclaim that centred round the Clermont Club. The other was that of a man increasingly obsessed with wild animals.

After 1976, the Wild Animals Protection Act placed serious restrictions on the trade in and ownership of wild animals, making it virtually impossible for anyone to act as Aspinall had in 1957. Then there was still a relatively free trade in wild animals, and Mr Palmer had no problem finding him companions for Dead Loss the monkey. First came the two Himalayan bears, Esau and Ayesha. Aspinall never had trouble from the police over the bears when he started keeping them in his ground-floor maisonette in the middle of Belgravia. Nor, strangely enough, did he have any complaints from his neighbours. Trouble only started when he tried to treat his bears like human beings.

Despite their cosy image, bears are not cosy animals. Even today the only way that Turkish gypsies have of turning their Anatolian mountain bears into pets, with whom they dance and wrestle to earn money from the tourists is to break their ribs and extract their claws and teeth while they are cubs. This was not what Aspinall had in mind for Esau or Ayesha, and rather than get rid of them he confined them to a cage in his back garden.

He had bought the bears when they were still quite young. This convinced him that, if only he had a chance to bond with a wild animal in infancy, the close relationship he longed for could continue when the animal was fully grown. Once more, Mr Palmer came to his assistance when he found him his tiger cub, Tara. Tara had been born nine weeks earlier in Edinburgh Zoo and Mr Palmer charged Aspinall £200 for the privilege of owning her.

It says much for John Aspinall's growing passion for wild animals that Tara continued sleeping every night in the Aspinalls' bed for the next eighteen months. It must have come as a relief for Jane when he eventually bought Howletts.

A year-and-a-half's close contact with his adolescent tigress had convinced him that, as usual, he was right, and although at Howletts Tara had to sleep in a comfortable cage near the house, he and his tigress appear to have developed the sort of closeness he had always wanted with a wild animal.

Whenever he found himself at Howletts he would always visit her, groom her, feed her and play with her. He claimed he could communicate with her, and grew to love her as he loved few human beings.

While he was settling Tara into Howletts and building a den for Esau and Ayesha, he was also making friends with another creature who would play a crucial part in his life with animals – the gorilla. This began at London Zoo when, like many visitors, he became fascinated by the zoo's star attraction of the day, the famous old silverback male gorilla, Guy. Impressed by his dignity and pitying him for what he felt must be his boredom, he began visiting Guy regularly. Soon, thanks to a friendly keeper, he was permitted to make Guy offerings of vegetables and fruit. According to Brian Masters, it was then that he formed 'the romantic, absurd notion that one day he would count an adult, male gorilla as his friend.'

Once he had moved to Howletts this notion was absurd no longer. Soon after moving in, Aspinall paid £1,700 for a young male gorilla called Kivu. Like many gorillas captured in the wild, Kivu had been badly treated by his captors and Aspinall understood that what he needed was, above all, tender loving care. Who better to provide it than his mother-in-law, the widowed Mrs Hastings who was living in a cottage on the estate? She soon became devoted to Kivu and, following her son-in-law's example with Tara, Mrs Hastings would sometimes share her bed with him at night. Sadly even this was not enough. Kivu was suffering from the primate's equivalent of post-traumatic stress disorder after losing his own mother. He sank into melancholy, and died a few months later.

Kivu's death affected Aspinall profoundly, but he also saw it as a challenge. Within a month or two he bought a pair of gorillas, a male called Gugis and a female called Shamba. This time he was determined to succeed, and hoped that, given time, Gugis and Shamba would become one of the very first pairs of gorillas to breed in captivity. His enthusiasm for his animals did not stop there. Discovering that wolves were once indigenous in Britain he bought a male and a female, hoping they too would breed and he could have a wolf pack of his own at Howletts.

But already he was having fresh problems with his two brown bears when he tried to let them wander freely around the grounds. After complaints from neighbouring farmers, he realised that Esau and Ayesha had to be enclosed, but even when they were, he went on trying to make friends with them. It wasn't easy. Once, when he thoughtlessly entered the bears' enclosure while they were copulating, Esau understandably took offence and came at him with a speed and fury he never expected. He was lucky to escape with his life. So was Lady Osborne when she tried to make friends with the fully grown male wolf. She was rescued just as he was about to bite her throat out, but like her son, she emerged unfazed from the experience.

Although in terms of friendship both the wolves and the bears had proved a disappointment, Tara the tiger and the gorillas Gugis and Shamba, more than made up for this. All those months of bonding evidently worked. The trust between Aspinall and Tara seemed stronger than ever, while his relations with the two gorillas had achieved a point of almost casual sociability. He played with them, wrestled with them and brought the finest food down from the Clermont for them. Unlike some of the gamblers at the Clermont, his animals never bored him and he studied them and tried to understand them. Slowly he started to believe that he was entering their private world. There were times when he felt he was becoming some sort of wild animal himself.

'Sometimes when I'm pleased to meet a friend, I find myself purring like a tiger. When I make love I even grunt like a gorilla,' he wrote.

The sense of power and empathy he felt he had with wild animals could be dangerous. James Osborne remembers one night on safari in the Serengeti when a large male lion started roaring angrily outside the camp and they had to physically restrain Aspinall from going out to reason with him. Undoubtedly along with the sympathy he felt for all wild animals went an element of sheer bravado. Just as the essence of gambling lies in taking risks, so his greatest admiration went to those who faced the greatest dangers. In himself he was always challenged by the need to overcome whatever fear he may have felt in the presence of a wild animal.

He was lucky in possessing such a dominating personality. The same charisma that appeared to work so well with his gamblers also worked with animals. He unquestionably had a remarkable way with them and, natural exhibitionist that he was, could rarely resist showing it. Several times he took Tara to the Clermont where she used to pad up and down the grand staircase. When Gugis developed a hernia, rather than leave him to the mercy of the local vet he drove him up to London in his Rolls and had him operated on at once in a Harley Street clinic. The operation was successful. Afterwards he drove him back to Howletts.

Howletts rapidly became a rich man's private zoo. With money flowing in from the profits of the Clermont, he began acquiring more and more animals and he was now able to expand the place beyond his wildest dreams. A mate was found for Tara, and five new tiger cubs, including Zorra, were soon playing around the house.

As Howletts started to develop, one gets a glimpse of what really lay behind this whole extraordinary creation. At school and then at Oxford, Aspinall had shown signs of the strong influence of the two writers he read in adolescence, Oscar Wilde and Rider Haggard. Predictably Wilde's influence faded, but Haggard's stayed with him throughout his life. From Haggard's Zulu king Shaka, he acquired some of the unfashionable traits which never left him – aggressive male chauvinism, glorification of danger and pride in separation from the common herd.

But another book he read in childhood was possibly the greatest influence of all, certainly as far as Howletts was concerned: Kipling's *Jungle Book*. There were obvious similarities between Kipling's hero, the orphan Mowgli, and the young Aspinall: both were lost boys, separated from English families in India, and one can understand the impact on Aspinall when he read of Mowgli finding himself a family among the creatures of the jungle.

It seems as if at Howletts Aspinall was doing something similar. Not only was he busily inventing yet another self, but with his animals he was clearly trying to create his ideal family. As with Mowgli, his first real friendship with an animal had been with a monkey. His efforts to improve on this with Esau and Ayesha were a failure, but with Tara he did something that not even Mowgli could do. In the *Jungle Book* Mowgli's greatest enemy, feared by all the other creatures of the jungle, is Shere Khan the tiger. In the end, Mowgli triumphs by outwitting him, but with Tara during those early months of bonding, Aspinall turned his tiger into a close and trusted friend. Once Tara had mated and produced her cubs, this family of tigers became part of his own extended family. Something similar developed from the empathy he formed with his gorillas, their children, and the rest of the great gorilla colony he formed at Howletts.

To have stayed true to Kipling, he should have been able to establish something closer still with Mowgli's greatest friends and protectors in the jungle, the wolves, and it must have been a bitter disappointment when his attempts to befriend his own two wolves failed so disastrously. But his relationships with his tigers and gorillas more than made up for this, particularly when he could teach his own children, Damian and Amanda, to treat the tiger cubs and the young gorillas like siblings.

Not all the members of the Clermont Set were so understanding over the Aspinalls' behaviour with their wild animals. Jimmy Goldsmith refused outright to have anything to do with them. According to Taki, 'Whenever he went to Howletts, Jimmy used to hurry past the cages without so much as a sideways glance at any of the animals. He told Annabel, "However friendly you become with a wild animal, if it is frightened or distracted you can never trust it."'

Mark Birley felt the same, which may have been why the surprise trip had seemed particularly exciting for the children. With the Aspinall family out in force to greet them, one can also understand why Annabel showed such trust in them. She had previously entered the tiger's enclosure herself, and if Aspinall and his children had no fears about entering Zorra's cage that April morning, why should she?

At the same time, one can also see what a disaster the accident with Robin and the tiger was for Aspinall. Too many accidents had been occurring recently at Howletts. During the last year, two keepers had been killed, and a month or two before a young model was badly mauled by a tiger and nearly lost her arm.

Because of this, what happened to Robin placed Aspinall in a dilemma. From the start, he had always encouraged his keepers to enter the cages just as he did himself to form friendships with the animals. The whole idea of Howletts was that, unlike what went on in other zoos, friendship and trust could grow between human beings and wild animals. If pity or remorse for Robin forced him to go back on this and admit that he was wrong, this could destroy the whole purpose of Howletts, and everything it stood for.

Rarely can Aspinall have needed quite so much of his famous self-control as in the days following the accident. At the Clermont, some of those who knew what had happened were shocked that he seemed to give no indication of being in the least concerned, and it was several days before he visited the badly injured boy in hospital. Four or five days after the accident, when he finally did turn up at Canterbury Hospital, what happened next seems quite bizarre even for Aspinall.

Robin had come through the operation better than expected, but although his life was not now in danger, it was clear that he would need several years of intensive and painful surgery to rebuild his face. Annabel spent the next few days doing her best to comfort him and one by one the members of the family came to visit him in his small private room. But the one visitor he longed for most was Aspinall.

According to Robin, when he finally appeared he seemed 'distinctly subdued and tense' which in itself was most unlike him. In an attempt to lighten the atmosphere Aspinall lifted up his hands to show the damage Zorra's teeth had done to them. This clearly made little impression on Robin. Some desultory conversation followed, and Aspinall must have realised that the occasion called for something more dramatic than mere words.

Without the slightest show of embarrassment, he proceeded to take off all his clothes, turned his back on Robin, and then did what he called 'a ball swing'. According to Robin, he had 'unusually attenuated' testicles. In the jungle, male gorillas wishing to show submission to another male apparently do so by exposing the most vulnerable part of their anatomy. By now doing the same, Aspinall was saying sorry in the only way he could.

Apparently it worked. Although Robin's face was swathed in bandages, and he couldn't hope to smile, he said later that 'the performance cheered us both enormously'. From then on Robin found it impossible to feel angry with him. 'Aspinall never apologised for what had happened, and I didn't want him to,' he told me. 'Even then I knew that once I started blaming him, I'd lose him, and that was something that I couldn't bear to contemplate. He was a great joy in my life. He was funny and a wonderful storyteller, and I loved him. It was as simple as that. So there could obviously be no question of suing him for what had happened.'

Because of the loyalty and love his injured son so obviously had for Aspinall, even Mark Birley, although still understandably furious and bitter with both Aspinall and Annabel for what had happened, felt obliged to go along with it all for Robin's sake. Having been told he would have to endure many more operations in the future, he would obviously be in need of all the love and support that they could give him.

In the years ahead Robin would have his periods of deep depression, but in the midst of them he knew that Aspinall had no time for people who felt sorry for themselves, so he told himself that self-pity was out of the question. Remembering this period he says, 'I suppose the truth is that Aspinall never had much time for the misery of others. His attitude was that if you fuck up you get on with life, so I did my best to do the same.'

So it was that because of Robin's devotion to Aspinall nobody around him dared to rock the boat by blaming him for the disaster. Annabel even wrote effusively to him several times to thank him for saving her son's life, and the bonds within the Clermont Set weren't threatened as they could so easily have been. Certainly it seemed Aspinall's magnetic power was stronger than ever. When I asked Robin's father, Mark Birley how this could have happened he replied, 'Aspinall had great charisma – unfortunately!'

11

Master of the Games

ONE ESSENTIAL MYSTERY lying at the very heart of the Clermont and the dramas now unfolding round it has so far been ignored. This is the mystery of gambling itself. What is there about addictive gambling that continues to attract so many people to so many different games of chance around the world? And in particular, what was so special about the gambling at the Clermont Club, and Aspinall's part in it? Apart from the lure of its exclusive clientele and the pleasures of Annabel's downstairs, why did it bring so many rich and famous people to its green baize tables night after desperate night throughout the sixties?

The psychology of gambling has always been difficult to explain, and no one has been very good at it. Sigmund Freud, initially fascinated by the subject, predictably decided that addictive gambling was a symptom of dysfunctional sexuality, and then gave up on it. Almost as predictably his disciple Edmund Bergler detected the workings of the Oedipus complex, and others claimed to have discovered strong masochistic tendencies in the psyches of destructively addictive gamblers. None of which gets one very far.

For what it's worth my own theory is that, just as gambling apparently grew from the use of games of chance to discover the will of the gods in primitive religions, so a lot of high-stakes gambling still resembles an addictive cult religion, in which gamblers entrust their fate to the fall of the cards or the turn of a roulette wheel, much as the faithful place their fate in the hands of the Almighty. The sacrosanct nature of the rules of the game, the stylised rituals of the dealers and the ultimate mystery of the winning numbers, all bring a touch of the supernatural to gambling. At the Clermont, Aspinall moved like a priest among his followers, dispensing happiness or misery through the mysteries of the gaming table.

Like many cults, this was almost something of a racket. Apart from enhancing Aspinall's own self-image, it of course enabled him to extract large sums of money from his rich believers. More interestingly, he became something of a guru to many of his friends and followers.

Once he had extended his interest from the gambling at the Clermont to his adoptive family of wild animals at Howletts, Aspinall's charismatic role increased, as he took on something of the power of the dangerous animals he treated as his closest friends. There was nothing particularly original in this. In simpler cultures, gurus and mesmeric figures have frequently impressed their followers by their power over dangerous animals. Christianity itself preserves echoes of earlier animalistic cults in the legends of the saints whose holiness was revealed through their relationship with wild animals, from St Jerome who was tended in the wilderness by a friendly lion to St Francis who expressed his love for all creation through the birds and wild creatures he befriended.

It was typical of Aspinall to identify with the most powerful and dangerous wild animals, and as he remained very much a gambler, the risks he regularly took with them meant that whenever he was in their presence he, and anybody with him, were consciously gambling with their lives. On the whole it was a fairly long-odds bet, but as one sees from the fate of Robin Birley, entrusting a human being with a grown tiger has to be a gamble just the same. Over the years five Howletts keepers lost their lives when the gamble happened to go wrong, and although Aspinall didn't advertise the fact, his friendly beasts nearly killed him on several occasions.

His body bore the scars caused by bites from his affectionate gorillas and scratches from his playful tigers. On one occasion, when the journalist Lynn Barber was interviewing him at Howletts, a fully grown African male elephant suddenly turned nasty, as African male elephants can, and threw him to the ground where it would have trampled him to death but for the intervention of the keepers. After his rescue it was typical of Aspinall that, though bruised and badly shaken, he insisted on continuing the interview as if nothing very much had happened.

When the Duke of Devonshire remarked that Aspinall was amoral, he did him an injustice. Far from being devoid of morals, Aspinall was a man who probably had too many. The only trouble was that he made his own morality – and most disturbing much of it turned out to be, particularly when he used his animals as models for his personal behaviour and his widely proclaimed political beliefs.

Having identified so closely with his gorillas, that he started to imitate their habits and showed a marked preference for the rules governing the world of animals to that of human beings. From watching how the dominant old silverback gorilla ruled the females in his entourage, he concluded that the idea of women's rights and women's liberation was not only ridiculous, but also contrary to nature. He also decided that an authoritarian, paternalistic set-up was the natural model for a human family.

From studying how the animal kingdom operated in the wild he reached some even more alarming propositions. The first of these was that just as the survival of the fittest seems to work in nature, so we should willingly accept the position of the powerful and successful as natural leaders of modern day society. He also believed as firmly in selective breeding for humans as he did for animals, and proclaimed that since animals had as much right to exploit the planet earth as human beings, the time had come to cull something like a billion humans from what he called 'the urban biomass', if the world as we know it was going to survive.

It was never entirely clear how serious he was in some of his pronouncements. Did he really believe that we should follow the example of the Inuit who, he claimed, used to leave grandmothers who were past their sell-by date outside their igloos waiting to be eaten by a passing polar bear? And when ex-president Nixon told him that a nuclear bomb would possibly produce two million casualties, would he really mean it when replying that this would not be enough?

Over one thing he undoubtedly was serious. Convinced that the earth was being swamped by human beings at the expense of almost every other species, he certainly believed that the concept of the sanctity of human life was an outrageous heresy. In his eyes, there was nothing sacred about human life. Given his guru status among his followers and friends, words like these undoubtedly had an influence on many of his extreme right-wing friends in the Clermont like David Stirling, who had started the Special Air Service, and who tried to organise a private army of armed vigilantes to oppose the miners' strike of 1973. There was also Lucky Lucan, who had apparently been brooding for some time on the teachings of Adolf Hitler, and who certainly had little time for ideas about the equality of women or the sanctity of human life.

*

In Aspinall's eyes the behaviour of his animals had also justified his treatment of his faithless first wife, Jane, and the way that, after their divorce, he had firmly kept the children from ever seeing her. It also led to the curious ending of his second marriage.

Although his second wife Min had devotedly cared for his animals, even acting as a faithful foster mother to his tiger cubs, she had always been longing for a child of her own. Finally she had a daughter, who was christened Mameena after yet another Rider Haggard character. But little Mameena had a congenital heart defect and died three months later. As her death almost coincided with that of his favourite tiger, Tara, it was hard to tell which caused Aspinall the greater heartache, when the baby and the tiger were buried side by side at Howletts.

Mameena's death brought something of a crisis to his marriage. Since Aspinall was theoretically convinced that, like his tigers and gorillas, humans should engage in sex solely to propagate the species, and he and Min appeared incapable of breeding, he finally suggested it was time for them to part. Min apparently raised no objection.

Since there were no children to fight over, and since, in contrast to his first wife Jane, Min had not turned against her male partner, the divorce was amicable. Min soon remarried and became the mother of three healthy children, but Aspinall was even quicker off the mark.

For him it was a case of third time lucky. His choice was not only young and pretty, but the two small boys from her first marriage had proved her fertility. Lady Sarah ('Sally') Curzon was the widow of a man after Aspinall's own heart, the young racing driver Piers Courage. Like Aspinall with his animals, he too had gambled regularly with death. Unlike him he had paid the price in a motor-racing accident a year earlier.

For Aspinall, Sally had a further attraction. Since she was a Curzon, her genetic make-up included traces of that 'most superior person', the great Lord Curzon, Viceroy of India and Foreign Secretary. After 'mating' with Aspinall she successfully produced a son, whom he grandiloquently named Bassa Wulfhere, after the grandfather of Alfred the Great.

He also decreed that at six months old, Bassa Wulfhere should be introduced to his friends the gorillas. Lady Sally entered the *gorillarium* and entrusted their baby son to the dominant female gorilla. The gorilla peered inside its nappy to see what sex it was then, with the baby tucked under her arm, swung up into the trees, and showed him to the other females in the community. When all the female gorillas had thoroughly examined baby Bassa, his gorilla mother brought him down to earth and returned him safely to his human parents.

After this Aspinall had no doubts over Sally's suitability to be his wife. Shortly afterwards he told his secretary at the Clermont to ring her up and inform her that they were getting married on a certain day. This was one occasion when the female was not totally submissive to the wishes of the male primate. Instead she telephoned his secretary back and informed her that not only was the day that Mr Aspinall suggested inconvenient, but that if he wished to marry her she'd like to hear his proposal in person. Aspinall was apparently quite put out, as he had been on the point of winning a game of backgammon. Later he did manage to propose, and they married shortly after.

It proved a lasting and a happy marriage. For

Sally, having been married to a racing driver, there were fewer hair-raising thrills, nor mercifully any repetitions of Robin Birley's encounter with the tiger. Although they made no further forays into breeding after Bassa Wulfhere, she turned her maternal instincts to nursing orphan baby gorillas. On one occasion Aspinall paid for a premature baby gorilla to be placed in the premature baby unit in a local hospital. Sally says that she never questioned Aspinall's intellectual superiority; in return he paid her what, for him, was the greatest compliment an honorary gorilla could pay a woman. 'She was,' he said, 'a perfect example of the primate female, ready to serve the dominant male and make his life agreeable.'

*

Now in his mid-forties, Aspinall was showing signs of calming down and enjoying married life. In 1972, he and Sally even spent a summer holiday with Goldsmith and Annabel aboard their yacht at Corfu. Dominick Elwes was there, with his latest girlfriend, Helen Jay. After all those debutantes and fashion models, Helen was something new for Elwes. One of the pretty Jay twins whose father

Douglas Jay had been a minister in Harold Wilson's first Labour government, she had studied sociology and politics at the new Sussex University, and was working as a current affairs researcher for the BBC. Elwes must have found this liberated young left-wing woman a refreshing change from his earlier girlfriends, while she found him funny, witty, and 'one of the most glamorous men I'd ever met.'

To begin with she enjoyed the equally glamorous world of the Clermont and Annabel's, where Dominick was in his element and something of a star. Most weekends they'd go to someone's country house where the spoiling and the fun continued with Dominick usually at the centre of it all.

But although she enjoyed Annabel's she felt less at home in the Clermont and began to find the atmosphere 'uncomfortable', especially for women, who tended to be treated with considerable suspicion. Surprisingly, the one person she got on well with was Goldsmith. He christened her 'the champagne pinkie' and enjoyed discussing politics with her. She found him very clever at defending the extreme right-wing views he shared with Aspinall and most other members of the Club.

Like Aspinall he took it for granted that the upper classes were racially superior and that the rich should be free to make a fortune without any government restriction. He also seemed to think that he and his friends were facing some sort of communist conspiracy which they would have to deal with to retain their rightful position in society. As Goldsmith had never encountered anyone seriously arguing to the contrary before, Helen thought it was a pity that somebody so bright had never had the benefit of a university education.

For Elwes the two years of his love affair with Helen included periods when he finally seemed to be escaping from his life in London and his dependence on the Clermont. Still hoping to follow the example of his father, he started painting seriously and he and Helen spent several months in New York where he worked on the portraits of a rich businessman and his family. Later, he took a job as artistic designer with a hilltop tourist settlement being built at Cuarton near Málaga in southern Spain. Here he was finally free to live an independent life, and while they were in Spain he met the drama critic Kenneth Tynan who was attending the bullfights with his wife, Kathleen at the nearby town of Ronda.

In Tynan, Elwes seemed to find something of an equal as a talker and an entertainer, with much the same attitude to life and a similar sense of humour. While he and Helen and the Tynans enjoyed Spain and made one another laugh, Elwes was a world away from his dependent status at the Clermont and was happier than Helen had ever seen him. In her biography of her husband, Kathleen Tynan summed up the two men's friendship: 'Dominick Elwes was a bounder and a wit and Ken adored him.'

But back in London Elwes soon slipped back into his old dependency on the easy patronage at Berkeley Square. It had been going on too long for him to kick the habit, and as usual he was broke. Painting portraits didn't pay the bills. Besides, he always needed company and an appreciative audience for his stories and his conversation. In the end it was this dependence on the world of the Clermont that ended his relationship with Helen.

As she says, 'Dominick was a wonderful person and I loved him, but I wanted things I knew that he could never give me, like a family of my own. The Clermont was his family, and I knew that it always would be. As there was someone else in my life by then for whom marriage seemed a much more likely prospect, my romance with Dominick had to end.'

*

By that summer when he entertained his friends aboard his yacht in Greece, Goldsmith was richer than ever in his life before. At heart he was still the same high-rolling gambler Aspinall had recognised in the sixteen-year-old boy he met at Oxford. But during the boom years of the late sixties, he perfected the technique of taking on old companies, closing their less profitable components and using the assets to build up the share price of Cavenham Foods, then purchasing yet more companies. Instead of chemmy, where you invariably lost, this was a form of casino capitalism from which, provided you kept your nerve and skilfully worked out the odds, you could walk away with quite prodigious sums of money.

At the Clermont, he often played backgammon with an unassuming character in a woollen cardigan called James Slater. Goldsmith enjoyed playing with him for two reasons. The first was that, although Slater was a skilful player,

Goldsmith could usually beat him in the end. The second was that as head of Slater Walker Securities, Jim Slater was probably a billionaire. A highly successful 'asset stripper' and manipulator of stocks and shares, he had transformed the world of British business and made Slater Walker the hottest financial institution in the City.

Although he always denied that he was an asset stripper, Goldsmith learned a lot from Slater, and in the early seventies had an unbroken run of luck with a succession of deals which culminated in 1972 with the acquisition of Allied Suppliers, for £86 million. Following James Slater's example, he diversified his financial interests and began investing heavily on Wall Street.

As a good friend, he encouraged Aspinall to do the same. At the time Aspinall had a fortune estimated at £2–3 million, and when this ran out, he continued gambling on the American markets by borrowing. With his investments doing well he was clearly feeling optimistic, and since the zoo at Howletts was expanding and needed space for yet more species, in a fit of financial recklessness he purchased yet another run-down property – the enormous mock-oriental palace overlooking Romney Marsh, which had been built for the eccentric multi-millionaire, Sir Philip Sassoon, at Port Lympne.

More reckless still, and convinced that his financial future was secure, he suddenly decided to retire from the Clermont. It was never very clear exactly why he did so. He probably felt, as William Crockford had felt before him, that he had 'cleaned out all the regular gamblers in London of their ready cash', and had little taste for the new wave of oil-rich Arab gamblers coming from the Gulf. He undoubtedly found his animals at Howletts more interesting than their counterparts in Berkeley Square, and in a fit of misdirected generosity sold the Clermont for £500,000 to Victor Lowndes, the London representative of Hugh Heffner's Bunny Club. Lowndes supposedly recouped the purchase price in three nights' gambling.

One of the first things the new management at the Clermont did was to remove an original William Kent fireplace from the hall. The only person who complained was Elwes and within a few days it was returned. Later when Aspinall sold off the wine cellar which Maxwell-Scott had so painstakingly built up for him, it brought in more than twice what Lowndes had paid him for the club.

On top of this, within a few months Aspinall was facing a disastrous fall on Wall Street followed by a run on sterling. Like a wary gambler, Goldsmith had seen the great bull market ending and by ruthlessly offloading all his available holdings and property, including much of Cavenham, when the great crash came a reassuring portion of his assets was safely in the bank.

He had already warned Aspinall, of course, but as usual Aspinall had shown himself the lesser gambler. Suddenly he found himself facing bankruptcy. He supposedly earned £180,000 in a month at blackjack and mortgaged the house in Lyall Street, but with outgoings on his animals running at over £300,000 a year the outlook wasn't hopeful.

This was one occasion when his friendship with Goldsmith really counted. Now a multi-multi-millionaire, for the next four years Goldsmith became what Aspinall called his 'lifeboat' against the stormy seas of bankruptcy. Goldsmith could easily afford this, and later got his money back in full, but it changed the whole balance of power between them. The old silverback gorilla had been beaten by his younger rival. Henceforth it was Goldsmith, not Aspinall, who would call the tune.

*

One service Aspinall performed for Goldsmith was over his affair with Annabel Birley. By now it had been going on for nearly ten years, despite the fact that she was still married to Mark, and Jimmy was becoming impatient. Aspinall understood his feelings all too well. Like any potent primate, Jimmy wished to have children with Annabel, and since she was not far off forty, time was running out.

Just as Aspinall had encouraged their affair in the first place, so it was he who now brought it to its culmination. During a visit to Howletts, he firmly instructed Annabel to 'go and breed with Jimmy'. Such was his Svengali-like influence over her that 'breed' she duly did. A year later, at the age of 41, she had their first child, his third daughter, called Jemima. Since Jimmy had been too busy, it had been Annabel's husband Mark, who had taken her into hospital the day before the birth. Jimmy arrived later that evening with a ruby and diamond brooch and a sapphire and diamond bracelet.

Many years later, in the memorial book prepared after Aspinall's death, his goddaughter Jemima wrote thanking him for her conception, adding how he had 'persuaded and coerced my reluctant mother into "breeding" with my father in the first place.'

After the sale of the Clermont, the old members went on seeing one another. They still gambled together at Aspinall's house in Lyall Street. They still had holidays together, and they often met at Howletts. The regulars continued to frequent the Clermont under the new management, where everything went on much as before, but they depended on Aspinall as much as ever. One of them who was still influenced by Aspinall's mesmeric power was Lucky Lucan.

12

Lord Lucan's Last Gamble

IF ONE HAD to date the end of Aspinall's grand illusion of the aristocratic gambler which had been so profitably created in that magical house of William Kent's in Berkeley Square, it would have to be 7 November 1974, when somebody smashed in the skull of a twenty-eight-year-old nanny with a two-foot length of lead piping in the basement of a house in Belgravia.

Among many unexpected consequences of this grim event was the disappearance of one of the five original members of the Clermont Set. For although no one was ever put on trial in a court of law for what occurred, the Coroner at the post mortem on the nanny, Sandra Rivett, named

Richard John Bingham, 7th Earl of Lucan, as the murderer. This has been generally accepted as true by most, if not quite all, of those who studied or who were in any way involved in this brutal and puzzling event. The prime suspect disappeared within seven hours and in spite of endless speculation, books, searches and tantalising 'sightings' of the apparently homicidal earl in countries as far apart as India, Mozambique and South America, his whereabouts, if by some faint chance he has survived, remain as big a mystery as the Marie Celeste, the lost books of Livy or the crown jewels of Ireland.

Among Lucan experts, it was generally agreed that if anyone knew the answer it was Aspinall. In a short statement to the police he gave his own considered version of events. He confirmed that in his opinion the murderer was indeed Lord Lucan. He believed that he killed Sandra Rivett by mistake, and as befits a nobleman, the erratic earl had subsequently 'fallen on his sword' by throwing himself into the English Channel from a power-boat. Asked on TV what he would do if, by some wayward chance, Lucan hadn't died but entered the room at that very moment, he looked his interviewer Ludovic Kennedy in the eye and answered with uncharacteristic sentimentality, 'I would embrace him.'

Some years later, when preparing for the opening of a new gambling club in Curzon Street, Aspinall went further. He was discussing the décor he wanted for the club with his brother-in-law, the designer Anthony Little. According to the account of the discussion which Little wrote for the memorial volume compiled after Aspinall's death, he told him that he wanted to enhance the dining room with four bronze busts of his favourite gamblers from the past. First came his old hero, and the exemplar he had often mentioned to his punters, the greatest eighteenth-century gambler and hero of casino owners everywhere, Charles James Fox, 'who lost everything at the tables except his friends.'

His next choice, probably inspired by his wide reading of military history, was the Prussian Field Marshal Blücher, who lost battle after battle to Napoleon before finally turning up just in time to save the day at Waterloo. Third came General Gordon, who risked his life before the Mahdi's men at Khartoum – and heroically lost it. His fourth choice was odd. It was his old friend, gambler and murderer, Lord Lucan.

He explained his choice in the inscription which he told Little he had written to go beneath the statue of Lucan, stating that he 'gambled his life to repossess his children.'

Had Sherlock Holmes been a gambling man himself, he might well have picked upon this enigmatic statement as the key to the murder of Sandra Rivett and Lord Lucan's subsequent disappearance.

*

Everyone loves a murder mystery, especially newspaper editors and particularly when the crime involves a member of the British aristocracy. Since the murder, the story of the vanished earl has given the British media a wonderful run for an awful lot of money. Chief Inspector Gerring, one of the top detectives on the case, subsequently wrote a book entitled *Lucan Lives*. Gerring's boss on the case, Detective Chief Superintendent Ransom, firmly believed, like Aspinall, that he was dead. Muriel Spark wrote one of her weirder novels on the subject, with a Paris psychiatrist treating not one but two identical Lucans, both of them on the run. One was the real Lucan, the other an impostor, and the story ends with the genuine Lucan being eaten by cannibals in the Congo. The last 'sighting' of the disappearing earl to hit the newsstands was of an elderly banjo-strumming hippie recently demised in Goa, called Jungle Barry. Despite the fact that the old musician had spoken with a strong Yorkshire accent and had given not the faintest indication of a murderous, let alone an aristocratic past, the story filled the pages of newspapers for a week.

This ongoing fascination with Lucan's whereabouts has shifted attention from the more important and intriguing question of the actual murder, and what brought about the improbable death of the innocent, but sadly expendable Nanny Sandra Rivett. For the truth is that everything that happened, both before and after her death, was so interwoven with the culture and the later history of the Clermont Club that the murder makes scant sense when considered apart from it.

★

When Lord Lucan first entered the orbit of Aspinall's floating chemmy parties in the late fifties, he was one of the brightest members of what became the Clermont Set – an aristocrat, a stylish gambler (his distant kinsman Andrew Duke of Devonshire told me that he had the most perfect manners of any gambler he'd ever met) and the looks of a mournful young nobleman in a Victorian novel. Later it suited many people to label him a bore, but he seems to have been no more boring than most ex-Guards officers with too much money and an addiction to gambling. Aspinall must have found him sufficiently good company to have taken him off on one of his jaunts to Africa. He also had something else – a touch of glamour, so much so that another member of the Clermont, the film producer Cubby Broccoli, gave him a film test for the part of James Bond in the first Bond film, *Dr No*. Ian Fleming, who knew him and sometimes gambled with him at the Clermont, actually preferred Lucan to Sean Connery, whose face, he once remarked, reminded him of 'a Glaswegian lorry driver'. Fortunately for the future of the James Bond films, Cubby had nothing against Glaswegian lorry drivers, and Lucky lost his chance of stardom.

Although Lucan wasn't destined to become James Bond, he seemed to fit in perfectly with the lifestyle of the Clermont Set throughout the sixties. Indeed he could have been a model for Aspinall's ideal member of his club – hereditary aristocrat, Eton and the Guards, risk-taking member of the British army bobsleigh team, fearless gambler and man of honour (Aspinall described him as embodying the virtues of an Ancient Roman aristocrat).

He was a particularly close friend of Ian Maxwell-Scott. During the late sixties, Lucan and his wife Veronica, often took their three young children down to Gants Hill, the Maxwell-Scotts' big country house in Sussex, for weekends. In summer all of them enjoyed the swimming pool in the garden, and Ian and Lucan usually spent Sunday mornings playing golf. They were often joined by one of the Clermont's old-timers, another old Etonian, gambler and compulsive loser, the portly and bonhomous Charles Benson. Like Maxwell-Scott and Aspinall himself, Benson was a devotee of horse racing and earned a living as racing correspondent on the *Daily Express*. The Maxwell-Scotts would usually invite a few other friends at weekends and the Lucans seemed happy and relaxed in their company. Susie Maxwell-Scott had memories of the Lucans as a devoted and apparently united family. 'Veronica could be shy with those she didn't know, and she was obviously highly strung, but I always liked her and found her intelligent and good company.'

When Parliament was sitting and he could be bothered to take a taxi from his home at 46 Lower Belgrave Street to Westminster, Lucan would occasionally wander into the House of Lords. He never made a speech, but always collected the daily thirteen pounds a grateful government paid him for attending. This was the only money he could ever say he earned – apart of course from his winnings at the Clermont. These, as the easy years slipped by, became a diminishing resource.

Lucan was in his mid-twenties when he inherited his title and found himself with sufficient money to live very comfortably indeed. He now effectively had charge of the family resources, with no trustees or relations to nay say him. But the Lucans had never got remotely near the great financial league of families like the Derbys or the Devonshires. In the end this caused Lucan problems.

Like his old friend Dominick Elwes, Lucky was a spender, not an earner, and as the sixties ended, he was becoming dangerously dependent on the Clermont for physical as well as emotional support.

It is interesting that Aspinall never entered Lucky for the Suicide Stakes. Perhaps he realised he wasn't suicidal (although he would subsequently insist that Lucky killed himself). Or perhaps he felt he wouldn't see the joke, for by now there was nothing light-hearted about Lucan's gambling. Despite overwhelming evidence to the contrary, Lucky seems to have still seen himself as a highly-skilled professional, using all the expertise acquired from long hours at the tables to support his growing family. But although he was a successful back-gammon player who claimed to shun what he called 'games of chance', he could not resist the most addictive of all games of chance, *chemin de fer*. In the end chemmy defeated him as it defeats everyone.

His was a grim fate as his addiction began to bite: later and later nights at the tables and the slow sapping of morale, together with his remaining capital on deposit at Hoare's Bank. He could only have survived within the warm womb of the Clermont. Here he was safe from the vulgar world outside, here he could still feel comfortably at home among 'the Blues', those reassuringly familiar Old Etonians who were always there to joke with him or flatter him, prolonging the illusion of his carefree schooldays among all those other children of the rich. In that unreal world of the Clermont, there were always chums to make him laugh and reassure him that all was well and that by gambling he was doing what his friends expected him to do.

Besides, he always had the memorable example of his great-great-grandfather, the 3rd Earl of Lucan, who is still remembered as the commander at the most spectacular disaster of the Crimean War, immortalised in Tennyson's poem 'The Charge of the Light Brigade'. But Lucky's celebrated ancestor never let the loss of all those brave men under him 'dismay' him. Instead he soldiered on, becoming a Field Marshal and enjoying an irascible but comfortable old age. When he died at eighty-eight he was the oldest officer in the Army.

As all but the richest or the most insensitive gamblers discover in the end, it isn't all that easy to ignore the collateral domestic damage caused by constant losing at the tables. As his marriage suffered and his world began to fall apart, it was clear that Lucky was nowhere near as tough as his great-great-grandfather.

In *The Biggest Game in Town*, Al Alvarez's classic

book on poker playing, he quotes several seasoned gamblers to the effect that the wise wife kisses her gambling husband goodbye at the casino door and leaves him to get on with it. Annabel and Susie Maxwell-Scott both did this. So did Margaret Vyner, who recalls one evening when she broke her rule and, entering the great gambling room at the Clermont, noticed Lady Lucan 'sitting in the corner looking white-faced and hopeless, while her husband went on gambling and looking even more hopeless.'

It is not inconceivable that the reason for Lady Lucan's constant presence at her husband's side may actually have been because she loved him. Alternatively, she may have been jealous, or desperately worried. Certainly throughout this period she was always there. As Margaret Vyner noticed, once Lucky started gambling, she would sit behind him in her corner until two or three in the morning, at which point he would rise, bid goodnight to the sleepy croupier, settle his losses with the club cashier and stride out into the night to the waiting taxi, without a word to Lady Lucan who trotted meekly in his wake.

Taki, who should know if anyone does, says that just as there's no greater sexual switch-on for a gambler than winning, so few things in life are more detumescent than a run of losing. Sometime in the early seventies, Lucky's luck ran out, and he was caught in a downward spiral of despair.

He stepped up his drinking (not difficult with all that free alcohol at the Clermont). Simultaneously the money went on dwindling, then ran out entirely. When Aspinall unexpectedly sold the Clermont to Victor Lowndes in 1972, it made the unhappy nobleman's plight even worse. Aspinall had always been his friend and patron, and had more or less looked after him and financed his losses. Unfortunately Lowndes did not share this sympathy for the British aristocracy. Although house players had been declared illegal, Aspinall appears to have arranged for Lucky to be given the degrading position of a quasi-illicit shill in the club where he had once been one of its most favoured members.

Reports began to circulate about the breakup of the Lucans' marriage, with Veronica frequently appearing emotional while Lucky drank and went on gambling. One afternoon he took her out in his Mercedes. They ended up at that home-from-home for rich neurotics, cokeheads and alcoholics, the Priory Clinic in Roehampton. Getting out of the car, Lucan did his best to force her to remain there and commit herself for treatment. She angrily refused and insisted on returning home to her children.

The Lucans had become terminal casino casualties. He was now effectively bankrupt, and his wife seemed mentally disturbed as she tried to cope with her desperate husband and their three young children. By 1973 when the marital troubles of the Lucans seemed insoluble, no one had much time for this miserable couple. Then Lucky's popularity, if not his fortunes at the table, suddenly revived.

Strangely enough what brought about this change was the custody battle for the children which now began. The case was bitterly contested by both sides, and the judge, forced to decide between a gambling father and a mother alleged to be neurotic, awarded Lady Lucan care and control of Frances, Camilla and George. The children were made wards of court.

This fraught decision was greeted by the Clermonteers with overwhelming indignation on behalf of poor old Lucky. Unsurprisingly, the feminist movement of the sixties had made little impact at the Clermont, where Aspinall's philosophy still prevailed. If the female of the species resists the authority of the old silverback gorilla who has fathered her children, she must expect the sort of treatment that a rebellious female primate would encounter in the wild.

As Aspinall and his Clermont friends began to rally round Lucan, the image of the embattled earl began to change. He became something of a cause – an aristocrat and fellow-gambler whose life, home, status, even his relations with his son and heir, were being threatened by the one thing that, after drugs, communists and left-wing intellectuals, Aspinall most detested: an apparently uppity woman.

Soon Lucky seemed to be enjoying life again as old friends went out of their way to show him their support and solidarity. He even found himself a girlfriend. Jimmy Goldsmith, suddenly remembering his old friend, thoughtfully sent him an airline ticket and invited Lucky to his fortieth birthday party at his house in Acapulco. Annabel of course was there, and went out of her way to be as kind as possible to him in his troubles. As things turned out she was possibly a little too kind, particularly when another guest, Victoria Brooke (later Lady Getty) took some holiday snaps of the effusive couple.

Now that Lucan seemed to be enjoying life again, it might be thought that he would start to shed a little of the bitterness he felt towards his wife. If anything, the support of so many sympathetic friends only increased his hatred for Veronica. By now, Lucan had reached the rocky shores of total desperation, and a holiday in Mexico could not alter the fact that on the verge of forty he was bankrupt, in debt to moneylenders and had little hope of recovering his children. In his desperation he would cling to one supreme emotion – remorseless hatred for his wife. He had become a gambler with one thing only left to gamble with – his life.

*

Among his friends he made no secret of his feelings for Veronica. The part played by gambling and the lifestyle of the Clermont in bringing Lucky to this wretched situation does not seem to have occurred to any of its members, nor did Veronica's obvious unhappiness concern them. Lady Lucan suddenly appeared to them, however unfairly, to have everything that upper-class gamblers hate in the wife of a gambling man and fellow aristocrat. In their eyes she was dangerously unhinged and kinkily sadistic. Stories were told about the fate of a kitten – in other versions it was a puppy – which Lucky had sent round to the house for his children.

No British aristocrat would treat an animal like that, but then Veronica wasn't an aristocrat at all. Apart from being highly emotional, she was pretentious and déclassée which was worse.

As Veronica's state of mind grew worse and the whispering campaign against her intensified, her husband was not exactly in the best of mental health himself. Besides the heavy drinking, and his habit of relaxing with *Mein Kampf* and recordings of the Führer, this most courteous of gamblers had recently developed a tendency to lapse into uncontrollable rages when frustrated – as he often was.

★

Many ex-husbands have fantasies of murdering their former wives, but although the Lucans were still married, Lucky's fantasies became an open secret among members of the Clermont Set. Provided he had drunk enough, he would discuss them with almost anybody who would listen. He especially liked talking to the sympathetic Lady Osborne. Years later, she related to her son's biographer how Lucky had confessed to her that he felt that he had no alternative but to kill Veronica.

'And how did you react?' inquired the biographer.

'I told him he must do whatever he thought right,' Lady Osborne replied.

Later Aspinall told Brian Masters that, far from being surprised, that 'Lucan might have killed his wife, the missing earl had confessed to him some weeks earlier that he would like to do so.' Since Aspinall himself had not the slightest hesitation in later assuring the police that, had he been married to 'that woman' he would have 'bashed her brains out five years earlier', it is not hard to imagine what he would have said to Lucan.

Several other leading Clermonteers would later go on record as having been aware of Lucan's homicidal feelings. One of them, Greville Howard, (now Lord Howard) formerly Enoch Powell's secretary and yet another Old Etonian, who became a house player at the Clermont, made a statement to the police after Sandra Rivett's murder to the effect that Lucan had informed him that he intended murdering his wife.

*

Once Lucky regarded killing Lady Lucan as a high-risk gamble, he presumably relieved himself of much of the responsibility for what would happen. In a bet, one's actions are subordinated to the rules of the game, and in this particular game Lucky would not have seen himself as a murderer, but as a gambler wagering his life against Veronica's with their children as the prize. This may well have been the only way he had of resolving the nightmare that obsessed him. No true gambler chickens out once the chips are down.

As he made his preparations, he seems to have had no qualms about turning to a number of his Clermont friends for unknowing help. His most urgent requirement was transport. As his Mercedes was both conspicuous and identifiable, he asked a banker friend and Clermont habitué called Michael Stoop to lend him his spare car, a Ford Corsair, for a time, saying that his own car was unroadworthy. Stoop agreed. The Sussex ferry port of Newhaven figured prominently in Lucky's plans, and I have been told that he drove Stoop's car on at least two trial runs from Belgravia to Newhaven. On one of these he returned with a

US mailbag in the back. A friend from the Clermont had accompanied him on the trip.

Another important detail which was never really explained was the fact that Lucky apparently needed a considerable sum of ready cash. Since he was so deeply in debt he found this hard to obtain. In early October he made a hurried trip to see his friend Jimmy Goldsmith in Paris.

Scarcely a day passed now without Goldsmith and Aspinall talking on the phone, so when Lucky turned up at his mansion in the Rue Monsieur asking for a £10,000 loan, Goldsmith would certainly have known what was coming.

Shrewder than some of Lucky's other friends, Goldsmith was clearly wary of involvement and told him that throughout his life he had made it a habit never to lend money to his friends. He was, however, perfectly prepared to offer Lucky the one thing that he knew that, as a gentleman, he could not possibly accept – an outright gift of £10,000.

While it was apparently acceptable for an aristocrat to kill his wife in a high-risk gamble, it was not acceptable for him to take money as a gift. Lucky refused this generous offer as Goldsmith knew he would, and returned to

London. For the next few weeks, Goldsmith lay low in Paris, keeping very clear of whatever it was that Lucky was up to. As for Lucky there was no alternative but to make do with the best offer he could get from an unsuspecting Clermont friend, Taki, who was prepared to lend him £3,000. Several other friends rallied round and made the sum up to the £10,000 he apparently needed. Taki knew that he might never get his money back, but since the money was only lent, Lucky's honour stayed unblemished.

★

Now that Lucan had embarked upon the gamble of his life, nothing would be left to chance as he set about working out the perfect murder. Veronica had to disappear without trace so that no suspicion would fall on him, and he could instantly pick up a new, untroubled life with his children. Such was his aim and such was the stake in Lucan's final gamble.

Having considered various ways of achieving what he wanted, he decided that his best hope was to kill Veronica at home one evening, when the children were safely in their beds at the top of the house. The children had already told him that

Sandra Rivett always took Thursday evenings off. He remembered that after putting the children to bed at 8.30, his wife liked to settle down to watch television with a cup of tea. On Nanny's night off, Veronica would go down to the kitchen in the basement and make the tea herself.

He had checked that Veronica hadn't changed the Yale lock on the front door, and as he still had his own key, he would have no difficulty entering the house. He would do so shortly after 8.00, and wait silently for her in the basement. To catch her by surprise, he would stay in the kitchen in the dark, having removed the light bulb from above the kitchen staircase. The moment she came down the stairs in the darkness was the moment he would strike.

He must have considered using a gun. He was a good shot, and it was known that he kept an automatic pistol in a drawer in his desk, but the noise of shooting might alarm the children, and apart from the blood, forensic tests could trace the bullet back to him. Instead he chose a simpler method which he thought would leave no trace at all. All that was required was a hand across the mouth, a sharp blow to the head with a heavy instrument, then death by strangulation.

This still left one important point to which he evidently gave a lot of thought – the disposal of the body. This was of absolute importance for his gamble to succeed. If he left Veronica's body for Sandra Rivett to discover later that evening, he would be the obvious suspect for her murder, but if he could remove her body, together with all traces of the killing, the police would have their work cut out to prove anything against him.

This was where the mailbag came in. Fortunately for his plans, Veronica was small and weighed next to nothing. So when the job was done, it would be a relatively simple matter to make sure he had left no telltale traces on the kitchen floor, shove what was left of Veronica into the mailbag, together with the murder weapon, and quickly leave the house. He would have parked the Corsair close to the house and put the mailbag in the boot. And there it could remain until he was ready to drive it to its final destination.

The intended destination was something else that the detectives working on the case failed to discover. In fact it was here that Lucky's murder plans began to show a touch of unexpected ingenuity. When he asked Michael Stoop for the loan of his Corsair there was considerably more to it than simply wanting a less conspicuous vehicle than his customary Mercedes. The Corsair was to play an all-important part in his alibi. The idea was that he would make sure he was seen driving his Mercedes past the Clermont shortly before the murder. Having done this, he would drive to wherever he had parked the Corsair, exchange cars, and leave the Corsair at a convenient distance from Lower Belgrave Street.

If everything went to plan, he would have finished murdering his wife by 9.00, and with her body in the boot, he would have driven back in the Corsair to his Mercedes. Here he would once again swap cars, return to his flat in nearby Elizabeth Street, wash, change, and be back at the Clermont by 9.30 at the latest. At the Clermont he would have previously booked a table for a group of friends and invited them to dine with him. He would easily have time to join them for dinner as arranged and, if the police questioned him about his movements, he could say that he had just been dining with his friends before going home to bed at 11.30.

In fact he wouldn't go to bed, because he knew he had one final task to do – dispose of the body. He had already worked out how to do this. Dinner over, he would in fact return to the Corsair, and after an hour's drive to an undisclosed destination, he would leave the body with someone he trusted to get rid of it without trace. He would then take his time driving back to London, park the Corsair somewhere convenient to return it later to Michael Stoop, and go to bed.

When Sandra Rivett returned to the house she would have naturally assumed that Veronica had gone to bed and not realised her absence until the following morning. Even then it might have been some while before Sandra thought it necessary to contact the police. The police were hardly likely to jump to the conclusion that Veronica had been murdered in her own house with the children upstairs in their beds and no sign of a struggle or a body. When the police finally did accept the fact that Veronica was missing and came to interview him, as of course they would, he would be in the clear. He had an alibi for his movements on the night of the murder, and felt he would have little difficulty convincing the police that Veronica had mental problems. They were on record anyhow, and few who knew her would be particularly surprised to hear that she had left the house without telling anyone. He would tell the police that she had often acted strangely in the past, but would almost certainly return.

*

As a plot for a murder mystery this was ingenious, but as a blueprint for a real-life murder there were two fatal flaws from the beginning. The first was that the plot lacked any way of checking one crucial point on which everything depended – whether Sandra Rivett had in fact left the house. The other involved the chosen mode of homicide. Although he had rejected the idea of shooting because of the noise and the evidence that it would leave behind, he had obviously never hit anyone on the head with a heavy weapon in his life. Had he done so he would have known how hard it is to strike anyone a lethal blow to the head and not leave behind indelible traces of murder.

On both these counts, on the night of the murder Lucan's planning proved disastrous. Sandra Rivett had not taken her customary night off and just before 9.00 it was she, not Veronica who came bustling down the stairs to make the tea. She was roughly the same height and build as Veronica, and in the dark it was not entirely surprising that he mistook her for his wife. When he hit her on the head with the two feet of lead piping he had prepared, he was so pent up with anticipation that he can't have realised his strength, or the effect the blow would have upon a woman's unprotected skull. In the frenzy of the moment, he struck her more than once, and struck so hard that the skull virtually exploded, scattering cerebral tissue, blood and bone fragments everywhere.

The killing of Lady Lucan which he had thought about so long, and planned so carefully, and on which his children's and his own future now depended, had ended in disaster before it started. Lucky no more, the 7th Earl of Lucan had just murdered the wrong woman.

To compound his error, when he heard Veronica coming down the stairs from the sitting room to find out what was going on, he started attacking her as well, hitting her around the head as he had Sandra Rivett. Somehow she managed to slide down between his legs and grabbed his balls. The agonising pain made him stop, and suddenly he seemed to come to his senses and realised too late what he was doing. This was not a gamble or a lethal fantasy. He had just battered to death his children's nanny, and was now doing his best to do the same to their mother.

This was the point at which Lucan did something that seems so incredible in the middle of a bloody murder that it actually becomes credible. He apologised to his intended victim. He did more. He sat Veronica down, and found himself telling her that they must talk and try to work things out. Then, noticing that blood was pouring down her face, he went to the bathroom to fetch a towel to help to clean her up.

This gave her the chance she needed to make a quick escape. Stumbling down the stairs, she got out into the street and ran to the local pub, The Plumber's Arms, where she burst into the saloon bar screaming, 'Help me, help me, somebody's just murdered my nanny.'

From that moment on, everything Lucan did was an attempt to limit the disaster. Although his eldest daughter, Frances, had woken up and had seen her father and started calling after him, he didn't answer. Instead he hurried from the house and drove away. The police never did discover where he went. He must have felt it would be dangerous to return to his flat in Elizabeth Street, which would be the first place the police would look for him, but he must have gone to somebody who knew him, who wouldn't ask questions and who helped to clean him up. While he was there he also used the telephone to ring his mother, telling her that 'a terrible accident' had just happened at his house, and for God's sake would she hurry round to Lower Belgrave Street and take the children home with her.

Apart from establishing that this call was made from a private subscriber and not from a public telephone, the police were unable to trace it. One thing is absolutely certain: within an hour of killing Sandra Rivett, as well as finding someone to clean him up and help remove the bloodstains from his clothes, Lucan must have also got in touch with somebody who advised him how to avoid being caught by the police. At around 10.00 he left London for the coast, once more driving the Corsair down the now familiar road to Newhaven. But instead of driving there direct, he branched off along another road that he also knew well. It led to Gants Hill House in Uckfield where he wanted to talk to his old friend, Ian Maxwell-Scott.

13

'I'll lie doggo for a bit'

THAT EVENING Ian Maxwell-Scott drank more than usual, and after dinner he telephoned his wife to tell her that, rather than risk driving home, he'd sleep at the Clermont and come home next morning in time for breakfast. Over the years this was something Susie Maxwell-Scott had learned to live with, so shortly after 10.00 she went to bed, and was actually asleep when the doorbell woke her. She turned on the light and went to the window. Surprised, she saw her old friend Lucky Lucan was outside, so she went downstairs in her dressing gown and let him in. From the hall clock she saw that it was a few minutes past 11.00.

She told me later that her first thought was that

once again Lucky had been drinking, then she realised he hadn't. 'He certainly seemed to be completely sober, but he was clearly in a dreadful state. Unusually for him, his hair was mussed up, and he seemed distraught. I noticed a large damp patch on the right hand side of his trousers but didn't notice any sign of blood.'

' "Where's Ian?" he asked me. When I told him he was spending the night in London, he seemed upset. Then he quickly said it didn't matter, and apologised for waking me. He asked if he could possibly stay for a while as there was something he had to tell me and there were a few things that he had to do. When he had taken off his coat and I'd given him a drink, he said, "Susie, something absolutely horrible has happened." '

As the drink relaxed him he started telling her much the same story he had already told his mother about passing by the house that evening and seeing someone attacking Veronica in the basement kitchen. As the kitchen lights weren't on he hadn't seen him clearly, but by the time he'd opened the front door, whoever the assailant was had taken flight and all he saw was his back as he escaped through the back door, climbed the garden wall and disappeared.

I always wondered if Susie believed this story. It was said that she was secretly in love with Lucan, and certainly she always insisted she could not believe that he had murdered Sandra Rivett. Probably, like several of Lucky's old friends and some of his relations, she couldn't make herself accept that someone she had known and loved could ever have committed such an atrocity.

The sheer improbability of the story also makes the hopelessness of Lucan's situation clear. If this was all that he could offer as an explanation to the police, he could obviously not risk giving himself up. He must have known this himself, and the true reason for his visit was not to make excuses to Susie, but to settle certain things before he disappeared. Still foremost in his mind was the one thing that had sparked off all the trouble from the start – the all important future of his children.

First he made another call to his mother, who seems to have stayed admirably calm in the circumstances. She told him that the children were with her fast asleep. She told him to take care of himself. Then she mentioned that she had a policeman with her, and asked if he would like to talk to him. 'No,' he answered rather casually, 'just tell him I'll be contacting the police tomorrow.' And that was that.

He asked Susie for envelopes and paper, and laboriously penned a letter to his old friend Bill Shand Kydd, who was married to Veronica's sister, Christina. He began his letter by repeating the same story about surprising the intruder, as if he were starting to believe it himself, but the purpose of the letter was to beg the Shand Kydds to look after his children. Even then he had to emphasise his hatred of Veronica, and how desperately important it was to keep the children from her clutches.

Susie was always vague about what happened next, and I remember wondering if she'd been drinking. When I asked her if he made any further calls from her house that night, she admitted that 'he might have done' but said she wasn't sure. Apart from giving him time to write his all-important letter to Shand Kydd on the future of his children, this visit to Susie had a more important purpose. Whoever was organising his escape at such extremely short notice would have needed time to make his arrangements with whoever was going to look after him. While he did this he must have known that with the devoted Susie, he was in safe hands.

He certainly had time to do this while he was with her. He even had time to write a second letter to Bill Shand Kydd, telling him about some of the Lucan heirlooms he should sell to help finance his children's education. Then he had another Scotch and water, asked Susie for some sleeping pills which she gave him, and shortly after 1.00, he left.

His last words, after kissing her goodbye, were, 'I must get back and sort things out. I must find out what that bitch has done to me.'

But he didn't do anything of the sort. In one of the letters he had just written to Bill Shand Kydd, which Susie's daughter posted later in the day, he had written two sentences that showed his true intentions: 'I will lie doggo for a bit. All I care about now is the children.'

As Susie Maxwell-Scott watched the rear lights of his car disappear down her drive, the great Lucan mystery had already started. He didn't reappear, nor did he talk to the police. As far as anyone knows, he didn't contact his family or the children either.

Some time before 4am on what by now was 8 November, someone parked the Corsair in Norman Road in Newhaven. More or less by chance, the police discovered it there two days later. There were bloodstains on the seat, and in the boot a two foot length of piping with one end bound with insulating tape. It was identical with the bloodstained weapon found at the scene of Sandra Rivett's murder.

Back in London, Lady Lucan's appearance at The Plumber's Arms had set in motion the swift sequence of events that marks the beginning of a full-scale murder inquiry. Following the landlord's 999 call to the police, a squad car arrived within three minutes, followed by an ambulance which carried her to St George's Hospital. Once the duty doctor had decided that her life was not in danger, her wounds were dressed, and she was heavily sedated. The police would have to wait till morning before questioning her.

While this was going on, Lower Belgrave Street was sealed off. When the officers searched the basement the first thing they discovered was the mailbag lying in the kitchen in a pool of blood. A glance inside was all they needed to confirm the grisly truth behind Veronica's panic-stricken outburst on rushing into The Plumber's Arms. Her nanny had indeed been murdered, with horrendous injuries to her head. By the time Lucan's mother arrived to take the children back to St

John's Wood, the police photographer was at work, together with a police technician checking for fingerprints.

Early in the morning, evidently tipped off by someone at the Yard or from The Plumber's Arms, the first of what would soon become an army of press reporters and photographers was on the scene.

The lunchtime edition of the *Evening Standard* trumpeted the story: 'BELGRAVIA MURDER – EARL SOUGHT. BODY IN SACK . . . COUNTESS RUNS OUT SCREAMING'.

During the days to come countless statements would be taken by innumerable policemen, details 'ascertained' then followed up with endless questioning, telephone calls and laboriously composed reports. Theories would be discussed, tried out and then discarded in the face of further theories.

Interpol in Paris was soon enlisted and ports and airlines placed on top alert for a tall, slim Englishman in his early forties who when last seen was wearing a moustache. At Newhaven, Sussex Police were interviewing anybody who would talk. Thanks to unusually stormy weather in the Channel, only one boat, the *Valençay*, had sailed the previous night. What passengers the police could trace were all scrupulously interviewed. No one had seen anyone jumping overboard.

At this stage much police activity was concentrated on discovering Lucan's body, on the not unreasonable assumption that he might have killed himself. Had they found it, this would have brought welcome closure to a case that was already showing signs of getting out of hand. A case as sensational as this involving members of the upper classes could ruin a policeman's reputation and damage his career. If only they could find Lord Lucan's body, the inquiry could be instantly scaled down.

Since there was no sign of Lucan's body there was no alternative to drafting in coachloads of police to search the whole of the Sussex Downs behind Newhaven. The body might be anywhere across several square miles of country. During the next few days relays of police started searching every inch of it.

Tracker dogs joined them, and for several days an autogiro was seen hovering above the Downs. Police frogmen were given the wretched task of searching the bottom of the harbour until they could confidently report that the noble corpse was not there either.

In the end they found a body, but it was not Lucan's. In dense undergrowth towards Ditchling Beacon they stumbled on the skeleton of a judge who had disappeared some years before. If only the body had been Lucan's, many anxious minds – and not only those of policemen – would have been put at rest. Lucky had so disastrously bungled this, his last great gamble, that few of his friends could feel entirely secure. Who could tell which among them might find himself accused of involvement in this ghastly murder in one way or another? And if Lucan were alive, and the police found him and he talked, some surprising people might end up beside him in the dock at the Old Bailey, charged with aiding and abetting Sandra Rivett's murder.

Apart from the actual murder, it was clear that if Lucan wasn't dead, someone must have helped him to escape. He simply could not have vanished into thin air unaided and alone. The way the car had been abandoned at Newhaven was in itself suspicious. Had he parked it there before going off to kill himself, one could understand him not bothering to dispose of the evidence lying in the boot. Once he was dead, what would a mountain of evidence against him matter? But if he hadn't killed himself, and was 'lying doggo' as he had said in his letter to Bill Shand Kydd, even at that moment someone, somewhere must have been helping him. As the days passed, with not a hint of Lucan's whereabouts, it became clearer still that whoever was doing this wasn't only very smart, but almost certainly had underworld contacts and expert knowledge of how to conceal a man wanted by the combined police forces of a continent.

With one of the five original members of the Clermont Set now on the run, a shadow of suspicion fell across the Club itself.

*

In the circumstances it was not entirely surprising that so many of Lucan's friends clammed up when questioned. If any of them knew his whereabouts they clearly had no intention of telling Detective Chief Superintendent Ranson or Detective Chief Inspector Gerring.

On the day after the murder, John Aspinall summoned some Clermont friends for a meeting at his house in Lyall Street to discuss what they should do. No one has ever said exactly what Aspinall decided, but one decision did emerge that would have long-term repercussions. Clearly intent on damage limitation, Aspinall sent what he considered to be potentially the most persuasive person to visit Lady Lucan in hospital and try to charm or talk her into keeping quiet.

The idea that after all the slights and cruelties that Lady Lucan had endured from her husband's friends, it might still be possible, with a little sympathy, kindness and a bunch of flowers from Moyses Stevens, to persuade this woman whose nanny had just been murdered, and who had narrowly escaped a similar fate herself, into keeping quiet about her would-be murderer, is so grotesque that it says something about the climate of unreality that still obtained at the Clermont.

Elwes must have realised this himself when he found Lady Lucan, lying swathed in bandages. At this he apparently burst into tears and asked her to forgive him. Not quite the way a member of the Clermont should behave, but then Dominick had never really been the sort of chap one could rely on in a crisis.

Faced by the police, other members of the Clermont set put on a better show. Predictably, Lady Osborne rose to the occasion, treating the detectives as she had been taught to treat impertinent colonials in childhood.

'Have you any knowledge that might help us find Lord Lucan's body?' asked Chief Inspector Gerring.

'The last I heard of him,' she replied, 'he was being fed to the tigers at my son's zoo.'

Susie Maxwell-Scott, trained barrister that she was, refused to add to the brief statement she gave to the police. Aspinall stated his conviction that his friend Lucan, having made a terrible mistake, had 'fallen on his sword like the aristocrat he was.' He added that he thought he'd probably killed himself by throwing himself from a powerboat somewhere in the middle of the English Channel, but couldn't prove it.

★

When London's modern police force originated in the late 1840s it was intended to achieve two things: the maintenance of social order and the control of crime among the lower orders.

In line with this, the structure of the Metropolitan Police force was henceforth based upon the rigorously class-based British Army, with the constabulary and NCOs recruited from the respectable working classes, and its officers drawn from dimmer members of the gentry who couldn't make it into decent regiments. By thus mirroring the strictly class-based nature of British society, there was never any chance of the police challenging the status quo, as they had in less deferential nations. Largely because of this, the moneyed and property owning classes had traditionally regarded the police as being firmly 'on their side'.

But as the police inquiries into Lucan proceeded, it appeared that they were nothing of the sort, and when they began searching stately homes and country houses on the faintest rumour, one might have thought the class war was beginning. The police searched Holkham Hall, home of the Earl of Leicester and then, when someone told them that the Earl of Warwick was Lord Lucan's second cousin, they searched Warwick Castle too.

Someone must have also told them that the millionaire oil man and Clermont member, Algy Cluff, had converted an old wartime bunker into a wine cellar at his house near Dover. Putting two and two together, the police searched the house on three occasions. Just in case Lady Osborne wasn't joking, they also spent a lot of time examining the animal cages at Howletts. When for the umpteenth time they arrived at Howletts asking to interview Aspinall, the butler informed them that Mr Aspinall was having dinner. When they insisted on seeing him they were asked to wait, and finally the detectives were shown into the dining room where Aspinall was having dinner with his wife, his mother and a gorilla.

Soon rumours of Lucan's whereabouts began to circulate through clubland. Some insisted he had made it to South Africa, where there were still plenty of fellow-admirers of Hitler to look after him. Others stated authoritatively that the racing driver Graham Hill had flown him across to northern Spain in his private aircraft, without explaining why anyone as level-headed as Graham Hill would have done anything so stupid.

In all, the police searched fourteen country houses and estates, without discovering the faintest clue to Lucan's whereabouts, and as concerns grew that some members of the upper classes might be playing games with the police, detectives started muttering darkly about being up against an 'Eton mafia'. When British policemen start using words like that, something very odd indeed is happening.

*

The investigation ground slowly to a halt in the sinking sands of Belgravia – and stayed there. However they had done it, Lucan and whoever had helped him had raised two fingers to the forces of Law and Order, and organised the most successful disappearing act since the smile on the face of the Cheshire Cat.

They had also robbed the public and the media of what would have been one of the most sensational murder trials of the century. The last time a member of the House of Lords was found guilty of murder was in 1760 when Lord Ferrers was tried before his peers for murdering his bailiff and hanged with a silken rope before vast crowds at Tyburn.

In our less colourful age, Lucan's trial could not have ended so spectacularly, since the death penalty had been abolished in England in 1965. Nor would he have had the privilege, also long abolished, of being tried before his peers. But had he been arrested and then tried for murder, much of that closed society around him would have been exposed, as the lawyers made their arguments to excuse or to condemn him.

Since it wasn't possible to hold a murder trial without a murderer, seven months later it was left to Dr Thurston, the Westminster Coroner, and his nine-man jury to bring the whole frustrating business to a sort of conclusion. Sandra Rivett's body could not remain in the mortuary indefinitely, and the inquest started.

The evidence of Lady Lucan was heard. The Coroner had extensive powers not enjoyed by an Old Bailey judge to reach a decision. Pragmatic by profession, it was not his task to decide or even comment on what had or hadn't happened to Lord Lucan.

Lady Lucan's firm demeanour as she gave her evidence contradicted any suggestions of alleged mental instability. A small, determined figure in a smart black dress, she clearly recounted what had happened up to the moment she ran to The Plumber's Arms shouting that her nanny had been murdered. The Lucan's eldest daughter, Frances, also gave evidence, followed by key witnesses including Lucan's mother, and his friend Bill Shand Kydd.

The purpose of the inquest was not to apportion guilt, but simply to decide the cause of Sandra Rivett's death, so the Coroner refused attempts by Lucan's family to bring character witnesses and an expensively briefed QC before him to attest to the state of Lady Lucan's supposedly fraught mind. Similarly he refused to hear evidence of what lay behind the murder, including her husband's motives and the influence and help, if any, from his friends.

At the end of the inquest it took the jury half an hour to decide their verdict. They unanimously decided that 'Sandra Rivett died from head injuries, and that the offence was committed by Richard John Bingham, Earl of Lucan', which legally remains the position to the present day.

In the circumstances this was the best-case scenario for almost everyone involved. By placing the killing firmly on the shoulders of Lord Lucan, that was that, unless he ever turned up in person to face the charge of murder before a judge. One journalist present at the inquest was struck by the obvious relief upon the faces of some of Lucan's relations and friends from the Clermont after the verdict. When Sandra Rivett's funeral took place at Coulsdon cemetery a few days later, apart from tributes from her own family, the only other flowers came from the police.

★

It was left to the *Sunday Times* journalist and Old Etonian James Fox to quote a fellow Etonian who dubbed it 'a bad day for Eton'. In fact the outcome of the case brought considerable relief throughout the upper classes. Edward VII had preached the doctrine of 'not washing dirty linen in public'. In a full scale murder trial a lot of very dirty laundry would have been exposed. Whatever may have happened to Lucan, a number of people were saved from having to endure this embarrassing ordeal.

Lucky's last request to his old friend Bill Shand Kydd to look after his children ended up by being followed almost to the letter. Lady Lucan emerged from her ordeal so battered and exposed – not to mention short of money – that it was not entirely surprising that after a while she found it impossible to cope with the children on her own, and surrendered custody to the Shand Kydds. So Lucky got his way. He and his family had always been too much for Veronica.

The children turned out better than might have been expected. By all accounts, Lucky's son and heir, George Bingham, is quite unlike his father. He isn't wild, he doesn't gamble, and he has opted for the safe financial future in the City which his father so imprudently rejected in favour of the green baize tables. Recent reports about the hedge fund he manages are favourable, and if he isn't one already, he will be a millionaire before he's forty. He maintains his father's innocence, insisting that what happened was all due to an insurance scam that went terribly wrong.

As for Lucan, thirty years later his spirit still hovers in the limbo of those unfortunates who are dead and not dead. In October 1999 the High Court granted his family full probate and solemnly proclaimed, 'be it known that the Right Honourable Richard John Bingham, 7th Earl of Lucan, died on or since the 8th day of November 1974.' But when his son, George, applied to the Lord Chancellor to use his father's title, the Lord Chancellor, despite the High Court's ruling, insisted there was no proof that the 7th Earl was dead.

This makes the Lucan story something of a curiosity – a sensational murder case that turned out for the best for almost everyone involved, apart from the children, Veronica and Sandra Rivett, and of course, for Lucky. But Lucky was a gambler and he knew the score, and as a servant, Nanny Rivett didn't really count. If servants are so inconsiderate as to change their nights off, they can only blame themselves if things go wrong. Besides the Nanny's bad luck was in a sense Lucky's good fortune. By being there to bear the brunt of the 7th Earl's misdirected anger, she prevented him from murdering the mother of his children, which would have left a permanent blot on the honour of the Lucans in a way that murdering a nanny didn't.

14

What became of Lucky

I N THE ABSENCE of a body or an authentic sighting of Lord Lucan, it seemed that nobody was ever going to know what had become of him, particularly once the Coroner's findings effectively wrapped up the murder investigation.

There were several potential leads arising out of the circumstances of the murder. Why had Lucan felt obliged to make not just one but two trial runs to Newhaven in Michael Stoop's Corsair before the murder? Why Newhaven? And why, as one member of the Clermont told me, did he feel it necessary on his second trip to take one of his old Clermont friends with him and return with a mailbag in the back of the car? If he was simply anxious to reach the port by a certain time, why all this trouble?

When most people fuss about their time of arrival at a ferry port it is because they want to catch the ferry. But this made little sense for someone planning what was meant to be a perfect murder. Had the great Lucan gamble worked, and had everything happened as intended, the last thing on earth he would have wanted would have been to get to France, which could only have aroused suspicion. Even if he had been making preparations for the sort of unforeseen disaster that occurred, no fleeing murderer in his senses would have taken the overnight ferry to Dieppe. At that time of year he would have been dangerously conspicuous among the few passengers aboard; and since in those days the voyage could take up to five hours, the police would have had all the time they needed to contact their French counterparts and ensure that a posse of gendarmes was on the quayside at Dieppe to welcome the homicidal Earl to France.

But if there had been no connection between those trial runs and catching the ferry, what then? Why had Lucan twice visited one of the least charming seaside towns in southern England? Why did he have to reach it by a certain time? Why the mailbag? And if he didn't catch the ferry after murdering Sandra Rivett by mistake, why did he still park his car in Norman Road in the small hours of the morning after killing her?

In the midst of all the far-fetched theories that were soon appearing, questions such as these were such small beer that they were rapidly overlooked. And that would have been that, but for the appearance on television in 2000 of a celebrated South London criminal called Frederick Foreman. In the sixties Foreman was a man of considerable standing in the London underworld, who combined running a pub in Southwark, The Prince of Wales, with organising one of the most successful gangs in London. During the affluent sixties he had grown rich. Then, in 1968 he made one big mistake: as a favour to an East London gang, headed by the notorious Kray Twins, he helped dispose of a fellow criminal called Frank Mitchell, better known as 'the Mad Axe Man'.

Originally Mitchell had been something of a hero to the Krays, but after arranging his escape from Dartmoor, and then concealing him from the police, they soon realised that the mentally retarded Axe Man was a dangerous liability.

Foreman and an accomplice finally relieved the Krays of this embarrassment with alarming efficiency, and in 1969 when the Twins and their gang were put on trial at the Old Bailey for gangland killings, Foreman was tried along with them for Mitchell's murder. Frank Mitchell, however, had been made to disappear so skilfully that no trace of him was ever found, and the murder charge against Foreman was dismissed for lack of evidence.

This left Mitchell's ultimate fate as much a mystery as ever – until 1996, when Foreman published his autobiography. Believing himself protected by the long established rule of British Justice that no one can be tried for the same crime twice, he described how he and an accomplice had in fact shot Mitchell, but he wrote nothing of perhaps the most intriguing aspect of the case – the disposal of the body.

During his TV programme, still immune from prosecution, he finally explained how this was done. This involved what he casually referred to as 'a little facility'. This 'facility' consisted of the skipper of a deep sea fishing boat who knew exactly where and how to dispose of a human body at sea, so that it sank for ever and the currents never brought it up again. Foreman actually demonstrated how the skipper wrapped the body in canvas, weighted it with heavy stones and encased it in chicken wire.

Foreman's story reminded me of something I discovered back in 1969 when working on *The Profession of Violence*, my biography of the Kray Twins. Although the Twins talked to me quite freely, both before and after their arrest, there were certain things that they would not discuss, including what happened to the bodies of their murder victims. At the time there were several rumours on the subject. The commonest was that they ended up inside the concrete pillars of the Hammersmith flyover. My favourite was the story that the Krays had a hold over an East London undertaker, who as favour to them, used to place an extra body in a coffin just before a funeral.

I was never terribly convinced by either theory, and it was only some years later that a former close associate of the Krays told me what had really happened. This matched virtually word for word Foreman's account of how his 'little facility' had taken care of the body of Frank Mitchell. Like Foreman, he also said that the facility was in Newhaven, so while researching this book I went there to see it for myself. Once I started looking round, I began to understand the real reason for Lucan's visits and why he left his car there.

There are in fact two Newhavens. The town itself is split by the River Ouse, which enters the English Channel at this point. The east bank of the estuary is the Newhaven from which the Channel ferries come and go. It is clean, brightly lit at night, and consists of the ferry terminal, the railway station, various warehouses and a neat row of terraced cottages occupied by people working on the ferries. Back in 1974 there were also extensive customs sheds which were brightly lit and regularly patrolled at night.

The west side of the harbour could be in another world. The waterfront here is formed by ancient wooden piles driven deep into the mud of the estuary, and at low tide it looks like a Thames-side scene from Dickens. This is where the fishing boats still land their catch, and vessels of all sorts are moored here, from trawlers and fishing smacks to lobster boats, and derelict fishing boats ready for the breakers' yard. In the seventies, late at night, it would have been a badly lit, distinctly creepy place where a boat could come and go and anything could happen. Even today it is hard to imagine a better spot for the captain of a fishing boat to take on board a body in the dead of night, and then dispose of it at sea.

For anyone trying to devise a perfect murder, in which the victim's body disappeared without a trace, this would have been the answer, and is the only possible explanation as to why Lucan took so much trouble coming to such an unlikely place on those two occasions just before the murder. It would also explain why he bothered with the mailbag, and got as far as shoving Sandra Rivett's freshly murdered body inside it, before realising his disastrous mistake.

There was also one crucial fact about that mail-bag that nobody appeared to notice at the time. The all-important point was that this was an *American* mailbag. British GPO mailbags are much smaller than those used by the US Postal Service, and would not have been large enough to take the body of a grown woman. But although the American post office from time to time does sell off its unwanted mailbags through wholesale outlets in the States, and they occasionally find their way to surplus shops in Britain, they are far from being readily available in London. When they are sold here they tend to be sold in bulk to companies in need of a strong and simple form of packaging – or to someone requiring an easy way of wrapping up a body in strong canvas.

It is most unlikely that anyone in Lucan's walk of life would have dreamt of using a surplus US mailbag to dispose of a body. The mailbag into which he shoved Sandra Rivett's body would almost certainly have been the one he brought back in the back of the Corsair after that second trial run to Newhaven with his friend from the Clermont. One can only think that someone connected with the facility gave him the mailbag when they were finalising their arrangements.

Lucky's anxiety over timing his arrival can have had no connection with the departure of the ferry. What really mattered to him was that he arrived in time, with Lady Lucan's body safely in the mailbag, for the skipper to wrap it in chicken wire, weigh it down with heavy stones, then catch the early morning tide. Since such services did not come cheap, and a cheque would not have been acceptable, this also explains why Lucky had to rustle up that ready cash.

In the midst of his careful planning for his perfect crime, the idea of using the facility at Newhaven to dispose of his wife's body suggests the involvement of someone with the sort of criminal expertise that Lucky obviously lacked. Disposing of bodies is not something you can look up in the *Yellow Pages*, and certainly neither he, nor any of his fellow gamblers from the Clermont, would have known anything about it. This can only mean that someone from outside their immediate circle must have been advising him. At some point this person must have also vouched for Lucky to the owner of the boat as someone he could trust.

Whoever may have been Lucky's adviser, it is almost certain that, at this stage of events, this would have been the full extent of his participation in the plans for Lady Lucan's murder. Apart from making arrangements with the skipper of the boat, he wasn't needed, if only because Lucky seems to have believed that he had covered every possible eventuality himself. But once disaster struck, and Lucky's careful planning came to nought, it would have been a different matter.

As Susie Maxwell-Scott made clear, by the time Lucky reached her house that night he was in no fit state to think coherently, let alone to organise his escape and disappearance so effectively. After the shock of discovering his mistake he seems to have been in denial over what had happened. Not having planned for what occurred, he had clearly lost his nerve and at this crucial moment a new, decisive intelligence was required to save him. Either before or after arriving at the Maxwell-Scotts' house, somebody he trusted must have made a number of snap decisions for him.

One of these decisions involved him driving the car on from Uckfield to Newhaven as originally planned, and leaving it in Norman Road. Norman Road, where Lucan left the car is close to the West Quay, and while it is the last place in Newhaven where one would choose to park a car before catching the ferry, it is only a few minutes' walk from the waterfront. He unquestionably drove the car there himself. No one else could have done so at such short notice, in the middle of the night, and a passer-by spotted it there at around six o'clock that morning. Michael Stoop also received a letter in the post two days later in what he recognised at once as Lucan's hand-writing, telling him exactly where he had left his car.

Whoever was hurriedly making these arrange-ments for Lucan in the middle of the night, was smart enough to realise how sensible it would be for him to stick to his plans and leave the car in

Norman Road which he clearly knew already. Whether someone from the facility helped him when he got there is something else that we will never know. But long before the Sussex police had been alerted and had begun combing the Sussex Downs for his body, Lucan had definitely been met by somebody in Norman Road, then driven off on the next stage of his journey.

Through his sheer ineptitude it was likely that Lucan had placed not just himself but several friends and fellow gamblers from the Clermont at risk. If he was caught and made a full confession, as was more than likely in the state that he was in, certain members of the Clermont Set could have well ended up sharing his disgrace as accessories to his lethal gamble. With so much suddenly at stake, damage limitation had become the first priority.

John Aspinall once called Lucky 'my sixth or seventh best friend'. Aspinall had always been one of Lucan's firm admirers, and was a staunch supporter throughout his marital troubles. He shared Lucan's animosity to his wife, and like several other Clermont friends, was certainly aware of his intention to kill her. During a subsequent interview, Lynn Barber asked him outright, 'Do you think it's right for someone to murder his wife?'

Aspinall's reply was most revealing: 'Certainly, if she's behaving in a bad way. There are times when a woman can provoke a man and give him little alternative.'

Apart from this, everything we know of Aspinall's mentality, makes it clear that, to him, the bonds of friendship would have been more binding than the obligations of the law, and he would have done everything he could to help a friend before leaving him to the police. In Lucky's desperate hour of need, his old friend Aspinall was the one person he could have relied on for the advice and practical assistance which someone unquestionably gave him.

In that same interview, Lynn Barber asked Aspinall whether, had he known Lucan was a murderer, would he still have helped him? He replied, 'Well, I always think that if someone who has been a great friend, is then in a terrible position, you feel *more* warmly towards him because that's when you're needed. A friend is *needed* when things are going badly.'

But however warmly Aspinall felt towards his 'great friend', Lucan, it would have been difficult for him, when suddenly rung up in the middle of the night to have organised Lucan's faultless flight unaided. And since Lucan almost certainly ended up abroad, the brains behind his disappearance must have belonged to someone else with powerful connections in the European underworld. I had absolutely no idea of who this could be until one early April afternoon, when I visited Susan Maxwell-Scott in her terraced house in Battersea.

*

By then I had interviewed her several times. I got on well with her, and enjoyed her company. Every time I saw her she seemed frailer than before. She was tiny, and in old age had become strangely beautiful, with enormous dark brown eyes shown off by the pallor of her face. She was crippled and had difficulty walking, but seemed to treat her suffering as something of a joke inflicted on her by the Almighty. As a devout Catholic who knew she hadn't long to live, she was convinced that she would soon be reunited with her husband Ian. She smoked incessantly, as if anxious to hasten the process.

She enjoyed talking about the early days of the Clermont. She was the only person I met who still called Aspinall Jonas, the name he gave himself at

Oxford, and although she made it clear that she hadn't liked him, she still seemed fascinated by him. I had heard that in spite of his lifelong friendship with Ian, he had once banned Susie from the club when she was drunk and had burned a hole with a cigarette in one of his green baize tables.

Although she had previously told me in detail of Lucky's arrival at her house on that November night, she had made it plain that, like most survivors from the Clermont, she did not wish to discuss what then became of him. So that day I was surprised when she suddenly asked me outright, 'Now that your research is almost finished, have you discovered what happened to Lord Lucan?'

I shook my head. 'I'm still not sure,' I said. 'Either someone helped him to escape and he started life afresh with a new identity, or he must have killed himself.'

Instead of answering at once, she paused as if uncertain whether to continue. Then she lit another cigarette, inhaled deeply as she always did, and said. 'You're wrong on both counts. I knew him well enough to know he didn't have the guts to kill himself. And if he had begun another life abroad, I know that I'd have heard from him by now in some way or another.'

'But if he didn't kill himself, and didn't manage to escape, what happened to him?' I asked.

'Have you considered that there could be a third possibility?'

'Like what?'

She paused again, then looked me straight in the eye before replying. 'That he was murdered. Ian certainly thought he was, and Ian knew more about him and his goings on than anyone.

'So why didn't Ian go to the police?'

'In the first place Ian had no real proof. More important, it would have stirred up so much trouble for some of our friends.'

'So who murdered him?' I asked.

At first I thought she hadn't heard my question. Finally she nodded, then murmured a name I failed to catch. I repeated my question.

Again she looked straight at me, then in a clear voice told me who it was. Since I have subsequently discovered that the person she was referring to is still alive, I must call him Mr X. I asked her to tell me about him.

'Mr X knew Jonas well. He was one of those international money men who seemed to flourish in the sixties. He had connections everywhere. In the days of exchange controls, some people used him to get money in and out of Europe.' She smiled at the idea, and went on smiling at the thought of happier days when Ian was alive. 'I remember once when we were holidaying abroad and found ourselves cleaned out after an evening gambling at the casino. Next morning Ian telephoned Mr X, who told him to go to the casino cashier in a couple of hours, and just mention his name. We did so, and the cashier seemed to know all about us and gave us several hundred pounds of high denomination chips. This was one occasion when Ian and I did not gamble. Instead we took ourselves off to the bar and had a drink. Then half an hour later we returned and cashed in all the chips we'd been given. The money paid for the rest of our lovely holiday, and when we got back to London, all we had to do was to settle up with Jonas.'

'But what has that to do with Mr X's involvement in Lucan's death?'

'According to Ian, it was Mr X who helped get him out of the country fast and arranged with certain people that he knew, to have him looked after. Ian seemed to think that later there was no alternative for Mr X but to arrange to have him killed.'

'Why was that necessary, when he'd taken so much trouble to rescue him in the first place?'

'I wouldn't know. I suppose poor John just got too hot to handle.'

'Did Ian ever mention where he might be buried?'

'It was a long time ago, but I do remember Ian saying something about him being buried somewhere in Switzerland.'

★

At first her story struck me as unlikely, and although I tried talking about it to her later, we never got much further. What other facts she told me about the shadowy Mr X had little bearing on the Lucan business, but I finally discovered more about him on my own account. Shadowy he may have been, but for several years dating back to the early sixties, he seems to have provided an invaluable service to Aspinall and others. During the days of exchange control, when a succession of cash-strapped governments kept an eagle eye on the movement of money in and out of the country, Mr X was the man many rich people turned to when they needed to transfer money in and out of Britain. I even heard that he had helped Lucan bring some of his celebrated £20,000 Le Touquet winnings back to London.

Evidently Mr X's usefulness did not end there. His true skill came from his knowledge and his range of contacts among bankers, rich Europeans and that whole grey world of the international underworld. During the sixties this enabled him to trace a number of high-rolling continental gamblers who owed Aspinall large amounts of money – and presumably put the squeeze on them. The myth that Aspinall never pursued a debt was not entirely true, provided that the debt was large enough. In the memorial volume put together by Robin Birley after Aspinall's death, Angelo Baglioni, his favourite Italian croupier in the days of the floating chemmy parties, and later gambling manager at the Clermont, describes how he once accompanied Aspinall to France in pursuit of a notorious gambler who had disappeared after gambling at the Clermont, leaving large unpaid debts behind him. Mr X arranged for the gambler to meet them both in a Paris restaurant. After a short discussion the gambler agreed to pay up.

We also know that fairly early on, Mr X did Aspinall various important favours. Apart from growing rich operating between England, foreign casinos and banks, Mr X also enjoyed a considerable reputation as an international fence, specialising in stolen jewellery. The story goes that after her divorce, Jane Aspinall took several pieces of jewellery to the well-known pawnbrokers Sutton's of Victoria. This caused Aspinall considerable embarrassment when the pawnbroker, as required by law, reported the jewellery to the police, who discovered it was stolen. When they questioned Aspinall about it, he knew better than to implicate his friend, the invaluable Mr X. Instead, he replied that the jewellery had been a gift to his ex-wife from one of her admirers. As the police discovered later, the 'admirer' had been drowned in a boating accident in Italy three months earlier.

It seems that Mr X was one of those high-grade contact men and fixers without whom the shadowy world of international crime would find it hard to function. In the straight world he'd have called himself a business consultant. His knowledge was exceptional, and he was certainly the only person Lucan would have known who could possibly have told him about the 'little facility' at Newhaven. What was also obvious was that Mr X would never have done anything like this involving a member of the Clermont without first discussing it with Aspinall.

It is unlikely that at this stage Mr X made any further contribution to Lucan's preparations for his great impending gamble. Lucky had everything so carefully worked out he thought there was no need to involve him further. How wrong he was.

★

Lucky's behaviour after discovering his mistake bears all the marks of someone in a state of shock. This was all too understandable. He had suddenly lost everything. His unconvincing story of having interrupted an intruder was patently absurd.

In the state that he was in he could not possibly have organised one of the most successful criminal escapes in history on his own. Among his friends one man who could not possibly allow him to fall into the hands of the police was John Aspinall. He knew that once Lucan was under close inter-rogation, everything would be revealed, including the nature of the gamble, and the extent of encouragement and actual help he had received from friends around him. The world that Aspinall had spent so much of his life creating would have been destroyed. It was not only for Lucan's sake that he had to be got away – and fast.

Mr X, too had an interest of his own in keeping him out of the clutches of the police, having been involved with Lucan over the 'little facility'. Certainly for a professional fence and top international currency runner like him, it would not have been too difficult making the necessary arrangements to ship him instantly and secretly out of Britain. As much of Mr X's business was done through Swiss bank accounts, so Ian Maxwell-Scott's theory about Lucky ending up in Switzerland may well have been closer to the truth than I imagined. Once across the Channel, he and his minders could have driven to Switzerland within hours.

But once Lucky's new associates had him safely out of England and holed up in a safe house on the Continent, their problems would have only just begun. Within a few hours of killing Sandra Rivett, during his brief visit to the Maxwell-Scotts, Lucky tried to convince Susie of his innocence. Now that he had time to brood upon his situation, it would not have been long before he convinced himself as well. Once he had done so, nothing would have stopped him trying to return to England to see his children and attempt to clear his name.

Those who were hiding him would soon have had to cope with the dangerous situation faced by anyone who helps a wanted criminal escape. When dealing with an eerily similar situation, the Krays ended up deciding that they had no alternative but to have their former friend, Frank Mitchell, murdered. If Ian Maxwell-Scott was right, whoever now had charge of Lucan made a similar decision.

Whatever happened and however it was done, the ultimate responsibility for Lucky Lucan's death was essentially his own. By murdering Sandra Rivett and then escaping he had already signed his own death warrant. The longer he remained at large, the more he would have implicated others in his crime. In the end the reckoning would have come, as he would have been unable to resist making some sort of contact with his precious children.

Les jeux sont faits. Richard John Bingham, 7th Earl of Lucan, had made his final gamble and had lost.

*

By disappearing without trace, Lucky had saved his friends from the disgrace his trial would have brought them. He also saved his children from the shameful presence of a father serving a long prison sentence for murder. And in a strange way, because of the element of doubt that always hung around his disappearance, he also managed to preserve something of the family name. One could always argue, as indeed close members of his family often have, that the 7th Earl of Lucan was innocent in spite of everything.

Anyone who gambles with his life must be prepared to forfeit it if he loses. Lucky would have known the score as, of course, John Aspinall did when he wrote out the inscription that he intended placing underneath the bust of Lucan. Aspinall was right. As a gambler, Lucky Lucan really must be counted, together with Charles James Fox and General Gordon, as a seriously dedicated gambler who was also one of history's greatest losers.

Today when you enter Aspinall's Club in Curzon Street, the bust is no longer in the dining room as Aspinall originally intended, but in a more discreet position in a corridor. He must have had second thoughts about his original inscription.

Perhaps he realised it gave too much away. He replaced it with the words he spoke that night to Ludovic Kennedy on television: 'If Lucky entered the room now I would embrace him.'

But it was the original inscription that really said it all.

'John, 7th Earl of Lucan, who gambled his life to repossess his children.'

15

Alas Poor Dominick

THE LUCAN AFFAIR had shaken the society round the Clermont to its foundations – and the aftershocks continued. Most of the old gambling fraternity, who had gone on playing at the Clermont after Aspinall sold it, had now left for good. The staircase that connected the Clermont with Annabel's had been removed long ago. Increasingly Aspinall retreated to Howletts and the company of his animals.

Ironically, the two key members of the original Clermont Set who would be most seriously hit by the fallout from the Lucan affair were Jimmy Goldsmith, who had kept himself scrupulously apart from Lucky's final gamble, and one of Goldsmith's oldest friends, Dominick Elwes.

The first rumble of impending trouble came

when Godfrey Smith, the editor of the *Sunday Times* Colour Magazine, decided it was time for a fresh look at the Lucan story, and put his youngest reporter, James Fox, on the case. Fox was yet another Old Etonian whose great-aunt, the formidable Lady Astor, had been the first woman member of the House of Commons, but despite his upper-class credentials, he soon found that old friends of Lucan weren't exactly falling over one another to talk to him. The only member of the Clermont circle he faintly knew was Dominick Elwes. They had met socially on a few occasions, and Fox remembered ending up in 'paroxysms of helpless laughter' at his stories. He still rates him as something of a comic genius.

Elwes was also an ex-fellow journalist, having worked for a time on the ill-starred *Topic* magazine, and he promised to help Fox. Like many very funny men, Elwes suffered bouts of severe depression. He was also invariably broke, so when Fox offered him a £300 commission for a group painting of the members of the Clermont to illustrate his article, he was flattered and readily agreed.

In return, as well as talking at some length to Fox himself, Elwes spread the word among his friends that Fox was 'one of us' and it was safe to talk to him.

Several did, including Aspinall, who was particularly forthcoming. Fox also talked to various other old friends of Lucan, including Michael Stoop and Taki. Acting on his own behalf he got in touch with Lady Lucan. He got on well with her, and they talked at length on several occasions. He was one of the few people she had met who sympathised with her plight. After several weeks' hard work Fox had built up an extraordinary dossier on the closed world of the Clermont Set and the personalities involved in Sandra Rivett's murder.

When Fox's article appeared in June 1975, the *Sunday Times* Colour Magazine had a previously unpublished photograph of Lucan and Annabel Birley on the cover. Inside there was also Elwes' painting showing various members of the Clermont Set sitting round a table in the dining room at the Club. It was not the best example of the artist's talents, but one could recognise the faces of several well-known members of the club, including Aspinall, the Earl of Suffolk and a close friend of Elwes', Winston Churchill's grandson, Nicholas Soames. James Goldsmith was prominently depicted summoning a waiter.

Fox's article proved to be a fairly devastating exposé of the closed world of the Clermont, but it was the cover picture depicting Annabel, apparently gazing up flirtatiously at Lucan, that really caused trouble. It had been taken eighteen months earlier, during Jimmy Goldsmith's fortieth birthday celebrations at his house in Acapulco. Annabel, Lucan and Elwes were among the guests, and after lunch several of them had started taking jokey photographs of each other. Annabel just happened to be sitting next to Lucan and the photograph of her staring adoringly up at him had been part of the joke. Jimmy had been sitting opposite.

Since the photograph was taken, much had happened. Lord Lucan had disappeared, Annabel had given birth to James Goldsmith's two children Jemima and Zacharias and the last thing she or her lover would have wished to see on the cover of the *Sunday Times* Colour Magazine was this photograph of Annabel apparently flirting with a now notorious murder suspect.

That weekend everyone involved became seriously worked up, and started fuelling one another's anger. According to Ivan Fallon, when

Goldsmith saw the picture he became angrier than anyone had ever seen him. 'Goldsmith was a jealous, possessive lover, and this was not only a slur on Annabel but suggested that he was a cuckold.' Although desperately upset herself, Annabel tried to calm him down, apparently to no avail. One eyewitness described him 'striding up and down in a towering fury, waving the *Sunday Times*, gesturing at it, and beginning to shout all over again.'

Another person who was equally upset by the picture was young Robin Birley. He was now fifteen, at school at Eton, and still undergoing painful operations on his face. This had made him particularly vulnerable. Schoolboys can be notoriously cruel to one another, and Robin was getting used to taunts from the young gentlemen around him over his appearance. They already called him 'Tiger Birley'. Now they could tease him over the picture of his mother and her friend the murderer on the front of the *Sunday Times* Colour Magazine. On hearing of this, his father Mark became almost as furious as Goldsmith.

The question everyone asked was how had the *Sunday Times* obtained the picture? They couldn't ask James Fox, who was away on holiday on a

Greek island with his girlfriend, and who would not have told them anyway. But someone must have given him the photograph, and the only person Goldsmith in particular could think of was Dominick Elwes. Everyone knew that he had been talking to Fox, and they knew that the *Sunday Times* had paid him for his painting. He was always short of money. Who else could it have been?

In fact Elwes had had nothing at all to do with it, and had not even known of the photograph's existence. It had actually been taken by Annabel's friend, Victoria Brooke, who later married Sir Paul Getty, and was among a batch of holiday snapshots which found their way to Lucan. While Fox was interviewing Lady Lucan, he had come across it in a photo album. With her permission he had borrowed it, together with some other photographs, to illustrate his article. Michael Rand, the magazine's veteran picture editor, had picked it out at once as a striking picture for the cover.

But with so much anger in the air, somebody had to be blamed, and word rapidly got round that not only was Elwes responsible for the photograph, but that he had somehow 'betrayed' his friends by introducing James Fox into the Clermont circle in the first place. Unable to fight back, Elwes was an ideal scapegoat, and soon found himself banished and ignored by many of the very people he had dined with, and amused, and always thought of as his friends. Only a few stuck loyally by him. Aspinall was one of them. Before going off on holiday, Fox had in fact assured him that Elwes was definitely not the source of the offending picture. Aspinall believed him and did his best to calm things down and place the accusations in perspective. But this was one occasion when Goldsmith would not listen to him. When Aspinall tried to argue with him, he remained implacable. As Goldsmith was now his paymaster, Aspinall's old authority over him had gone.

'Dominick has betrayed my friendship. That's the worst thing any man can do to a friend. I'll never speak to him again. Dominick has betrayed me,' he thundered down the telephone. And that was that. Charles Benson also tried arguing on Dominick's behalf when meeting Goldsmith on holiday in Sardinia. He found him still so eaten up with anger that he utterly refused to listen to him either.

From then on the whispering campaign that started building up against Elwes was not unlike the witch-hunt which had built up in the Clermont Set against Lady Lucan. No one had a good word for him – and many still haven't to this day.

The cruellest thing about this witch-hunt was that Elwes had betrayed no one. It was all very well for these millionaires to blame him for accepting £300 from the *Sunday Times* for his painting. He had actually painted it in the Clermont dining room, where everyone could see what he was doing, and he had made no secret of who had commissioned the painting in the first place.

The fun of his company and the brilliance of his talk no longer counted. Over the years he had aroused jealousy and made enemies. He had always been too clever and too good-looking, and had sometimes treated women badly. But what made him truly vulnerable, within the company he kept, was the fact that he had no money.

In the past this could be overlooked, because he was personable, charming and by far the most amusing character around. He was never asked to pay a bill at the Clermont. He was accepted as the club's very own court jester, and traditionally court jesters have always had a licence of their own. Suddenly that licence was revoked.

Mark Birley had spoken barely a word to Goldsmith since he took away his wife, but because of the sympathy both men felt for Robin, they decided they must be united and teach Elwes a resounding lesson. For years Birley had welcomed him to Annabel's and recently to Mark's, the new club he had started in Charles Street, Mayfair, and had never charged him. Now, out of the blue, Elwes received an unpaid bill for £17.45, together with a curt demand for payment. Simultaneously Goldsmith wrote him an angry letter, saying that he never wished to see him again.

As the exclusion and what Old Etonians call the 'mobbing up' continued, Elwes did his best to fight off deep depression and ignore what was happening. It wasn't easy. The most painful blow of all came in the form of a letter from Robin Birley, bitterly blaming him for selling the photograph of his mother to the *Sunday Times*.

Elwes had known Robin from his childhood, and knew all that he had been through, the sufferings inflicted by the tiger, and the way he had endured the operations ever since. The last thing in the world he would have wanted was to cause him more unhappiness.

Elwes' last girlfriend, Melissa Wyndham, has

never forgotten how she went round to his brother Tim's Chelsea mews house in Stewart's Grove, where he was currently living, only to find him standing there, holding Robin's letter, reproaching him for what he'd done, and saying how it caused him so much misery at school.

'I don't think I can stand any more of it,' Elwes told her. 'I just can't take any more.'

Recently I asked Robin Birley about the letter. He replied how much he subsequently wished he'd never sent it. 'It is the one letter I have seriously regretted writing all my life.'

It was shortly after receiving this letter that Elwes escaped for a brief holiday to the south of France. Daniel Meinertzhagen, one of his old Clermont friends who had stuck by him, had arranged for him to stay for a few days in a villa at St Jean Cap Ferrat. At the airport Elwes met another figure from his past, the gossip columnist Nigel Dempster. Dempster had often written in the *Daily Mail* about his love affairs and his glittering social life, but this was now a very different Elwes who tearfully recounted what had happened and protested his innocence. Since Dempster knew James Goldsmith, he telephoned him shortly afterwards, but Goldsmith refused to speak to him.

It seemed as if, as well as his former friends, fate also had it in for Elwes now. His few days in France did nothing to alleviate his misery, and he decided to return to Cuarton in Spain and try to paint in places where he had been happy in the past. Within a few days of getting there he fell down a cliff and broke his right hand and ankle. Then he received news that his father was dying. He got back to England just before his death.

In the old days, when things went wrong he would have gone to a party, amused his friends and got on with life. Now he felt as if his friends had vanished and nothing seemed funny any more. Melissa Wyndham did her best to cheer him up, but she was very young, and his depression was something no one could alleviate. He spent a few days in the house in Stewart's Grove and tried his best to cope. In his heart Dominick Elwes knew that he had had enough. Hoping to raise his spirits, Melissa planned to take him off to Dublin for a short holiday on 5 September, and told him she would pick him up and drive him to the airport at around 5.00. Instead, on that afternoon, he took a lethal dose of sleeping pills washed down with whisky.

She found him when she arrived at the house

early that evening. Beside the bed was a note written by this man who had once been one of the funniest and most attractive men in London.

'I curse Mark and Jimmy from beyond the grave. I hope they're happy now.'

*

If James Goldsmith was affected by Elwes' death he never let it show, for by now, like a gambler on a winning roll, he was on the point of getting everything he'd ever wanted. With that magic touch of his he seemed incapable of losing.

Thanks to the gambler's instinct which had prompted him to cash in so many of his holdings and place the money in the bank, he was in a powerful position. Almost alone among the big financial players in the City, he found himself immensely rich and free to act entirely as he wished. During the summer of 1975, he was gambling for the highest stakes of all. By then his old friend and mentor, Jim Slater, had been getting into quite horrendous difficulties through improvident investment in the tempting financial markets of Singapore, and the whole future of the Slater Walker empire was at risk. Slater, dispirited and sick, was suggesting that as Slater Walker's major shareholder, James Goldsmith, should take over as chairman. But Goldsmith was in no hurry to decide.

Early in July 1975, just a few weeks after that infuriating issue of the *Sunday Times*, Goldsmith and Annabel were invited to dinner by her old friend David Frost and his wife at their house in Belgravia. It was the sort of discreet, high-powered evening Goldsmith enjoyed, particularly when he learned the identity of the Frosts' other guests, none other than the Prime Minister, Harold Wilson, his wife Mary, and his confidante and former secretary, Marcia Williams. In the court of Harold Wilson, almost everyone seemed to get a title in the end, and Marcia had been ennobled the previous year, becoming Baroness Falkender.

Harold Wilson had a disconcerting way of taking the most unlikely people into his confidence and giving them the feeling that he trusted them implicitly. He did this now with Goldsmith. On the surface this was most improbable. Goldsmith had never made a secret of his strongly held right-wing beliefs. He had been a keen supporter of Wilson's Conservative predecessor, Edward Heath, and had Heath won the 1974 election, Goldsmith even had hopes of a ministerial appointment in his government, which would have carried with it a peerage.

Wilson, a wily operator, must have been aware of this, and seems to have spent some time reassuring Goldsmith that, far from being the rigid Marxist he had been represented in the past, he was actually a good social democrat who wanted few things more than the chance of cooperating with an entrepreneur like Goldsmith. He also made Goldsmith feel that he regarded him as something of a financial genius.

Whether he really did or not, it is clear that Harold Wilson was behind Goldsmith when, early that autumn, he entered into serious negotiations for the rescue of Slater Walker. As far as the government was concerned, Slater Walker was so large and influential that its collapse threatened a serious loss of confidence in the City, particularly from all-powerful overseas investors, which could have landed Harold Wilson's government in a highly inconvenient financial crisis.

James Slater's extraordinary career as the financial *wunderkind* of the sixties, ended on 24 October 1975 with his resignation as chairman of Slater Walker. But potential panic among the money men was averted by the news that none other than James Goldsmith was succeeding him as chairman, backed by a rescue package from the Bank of England of £60 million. (It was later disclosed that the rescue operation of Slater Walker ended by costing the British taxpayer nearly £110 million.) Since the whole rescue operation was underwritten by the government from the start, it must have been done with the knowledge and the backing of James Goldsmith's latest friend and admirer, the Prime Minister, Harold Wilson.

By that autumn everything Goldsmith wanted was in place – social status, a vast amount of money, influential friends – and given a modicum of luck it should have worked. Instead, a chain of interlinked misfortune ended by destroying Goldsmith's dreams of power and splendour in cosseted anonymity at the top of English society and politics. The odds against this happening were so improbable and so extreme that one is tempted to see this as the moment when that curse of Elwes struck and changed James Goldsmith's life forever.

*

The first link in the chain was in fact already there in the *Sunday Times* Colour Magazine. For Goldsmith the cover picture was bad enough but it wasn't really that important. What caused the trouble was something that hardly anybody noticed at the time. In the article Fox included Goldsmith's name among the guests who lunched at Aspinall's house in Lyall Street on the day following Sandra Rivett's murder. Actually he wasn't there. That was all, a simple error, but it was enough.

After Elwes's funeral at the Roman Catholic cathedral at Arundel, a memorial service was arranged at the Jesuit church in Farm Street. It was an emotional occasion. John Aspinall spoke first. Understandably in the circumstances, he made no reference to the behaviour of the dead man's friends. Instead he launched into an elaborate oration, comparing him to an Anglo Saxon bard, and seemed to blame his fate on his genetic inheritance.

Then, something of the bitterness his death had caused began to surface. Dominick's brother Tim was so upset that he found it difficult to read the lesson, and it was left to the friend who had 'adored' him, his fellow wit and bullfighting aficionado Ken Tynan, to speak up for him, giving him something of the praise that he deserved. 'Even Peter Ustinov had bowed the knee before him as a wit and raconteur'. He said Tynan also spoke of how Dominick had squandered his gifts before those who simply had more money. But this was not all, as the congregation left the church, Dominick's cousin, the rugby playing Lord Rennell, was so incensed that he landed the considerably larger John Aspinall a straight left to the jaw, with the words, 'And that's what I think of your bloody speech, Aspinall.'

Aspinall simply rubbed his chin, remarking that he was used to dealing with wild animals, and the incident went no further. But the pugilistic skill of a nobleman achieved something which the eloquence of Ken Tynan couldn't, and made it into the early editions of the evening papers.

There was still no reason to foresee this causing Goldsmith any trouble. After all, his Lordship's anger was directed not at him but at Aspinall, and anyhow it had been a very small paragraph in just one newspaper. It was not the sort of press furore that one might have expected from the trouble that ensued. Nor would it have done so if Richard Ingrams, editor of *Private Eye* had not noticed the paragraph just as he was looking for something to liven up the pages of next week's edition.

Ingram's journalistic instincts suggested there just might be an interesting story here. Which unfortunately for all concerned, there was, as his reporter Patrick Marnham soon discovered. Almost the first thing Marnham did was to dig out a cutting of Fox's article from the *Sunday Times*, stating erroneously that Goldsmith had been present at the lunch which Aspinall arranged among Lucan's friends the day after the murder. As no correction had been published, Marnham and Ingrams had no way of knowing that he wasn't there.

A mistaken report about James Goldsmith's presence at a lunch may have seemed a relatively minor detail, but a minor detail it was not once Marnham started working on his article, which he entitled, 'All's Well that Ends Elwes'. It was enough for him to believe that Goldsmith had been present at that meeting of Lucan's friends the day after his disappearance. If Goldsmith *had* been there, argued Marnham, not unreasonably, such a powerful character would almost certainly have dominated the proceedings. More than that, with his wealth and his overseas connections, who better than James Goldsmith to then decide to help smuggle his old friend Lord Lucan out of the country.

It was clearly a hypothetical piece, and had Goldsmith been lunching off smoked salmon with his friends in Lyall Street that day, Marnham's hypothesis would have been perfectly reasonable. Since he was not, the article was clearly libellous, but because of the absence of a published apology for the *Sunday Times*'s mistake, no one at *Private Eye* had any way of knowing this. For several weeks following Marnham's article, the *Eye*'s financial columnist, Michael Gillard, otherwise known as 'City Slicker', began relating various details of Goldsmith's business affairs which other papers had failed to mention. The most embarrassing of these was the fact that when he took over as chairman of Slater Walker, and saved the company from disaster with public money, he was already one of the company's major shareholders.

*

It was never clear exactly why Goldsmith was so disproportionately angry over the article in a paper like *Private Eye*. Undoubtedly the picture in the

Sunday Times had already upset him, making him over-sensitive on the subject and over-wrought about the press in general. He had always treasured his anonymity, but must have been aware that by English standards his private life was somewhat unusual. Like most of her friends, Annabel often found the magazine amusing but, unfortunately, her lover didn't share her sense of humour.

At the same time Goldsmith had influential friends who thoroughly agreed with him about the dangerous influence of *Private Eye*, and may have reinforced his perception of the need to take action. Since their first meeting at the Frosts, Goldsmith had been seeing more of Harold Wilson. Each week Mary Wilson had been having to endure what she regarded as the tasteless humour of 'Mrs Wilson's Diary', which was written by the man Goldsmith now saw as the source of all his troubles, Richard Ingrams. Baroness Falkender had more serious reasons still for perceiving the magazine in a negative light since it had recently disclosed the existence of two children, fathered by a journalist on the *Daily Mail*. As for the Prime Minister, *Private Eye* embodied almost everything Harold Wilson hated in the British Press — its irreverence, its apparent irresponsibility, and worst of all, its dangerous habit of unearthing awkward facts at awkward moments.

This meant that, when Goldsmith made his final move he did so believing he had the full support of the Prime Minister. When he launched his libel action against the magazine in February 1976, he wasn't satisfied, like most rich plaintiffs, with any ordinary libel proceedings under civil law against the editor. Instead he decided to unleash a legal broadside of Nelsonian proportions. On 2 February his lawyers fired off not one but a resounding battery of sixty-three writs for libel, most of them addressed to the principal newsagents and distributors of *Private Eye* throughout the country, warning them in chilling terms of the legal hazards of selling the magazine in future. As for the unspeakable Ingrams, he found himself accused of the virtually forgotten crime of criminal libel.

This was truly fearsome stuff. The law of criminal libel had been used by Stuart governments against journalists they disapproved of, and the agitator, William Prynne had his ear cut off and was branded on the cheek with the letters S L, standing for Seditious Libeller. In 1813, although he kept his ears and wasn't branded, the celebrated editor and journalist, Leigh Hunt, spent two years in gaol for calling the Prince Regent 'a fat Adonis of fifty'. Unsurprisingly this law had become largely forgotten and was hardly ever used. Winston Churchill employed it to get Aspinall's hero, Oscar Wilde's old lover Lord Alfred Douglas, six months' in prison for suggesting that he had made money from the Battle of Jutland. It was also used against a journalist who suggested that King George V had been a bigamist.

For Goldsmith to invoke such laws against an editor like Ingrams showed, if nothing else, a certain lack of proportion. For him also to threaten the magazine's distributors suggested that his real aim was to drive it out of business. Above all his actions showed a fatal lack of common sense and humour. Did he really want Ingrams imprisoned? Was he genuinely wanting to suppress a satirical magazine which amused so many people? As Alexander Pope once asked, 'Who breaks a butterfly upon a wheel?'

During the ensuing months it was clear that Goldsmith did. His old friend Anthony Blond described meeting him soon after his legal action started. 'Jimmy became wilder and madder whenever I suggested he stopped persecuting *Private Eye*. "They have attacked my son," he said. "I will throw them into prison. I will hound their wives even in their widows' weeds." All this was most anxious making.'

It was indeed, not least for Richard Ingrams and the staff of *Private Eye* when Judge Wien in his wisdom decided that the case was so serious that Ingrams would have to face the charge of criminal libel in a higher court.

As too often happens with the English libel laws, Goldsmith was relying on the power of money to force his enemies into submission. *Private Eye* fought back in the only way it could – by ridicule. Goldsmith was not used to being ridiculed, so when in the next issue of the *Eye* he was christened 'Goldenballs', he grew angrier than ever.

He was angrier still when *Private Eye* began what it called 'the Goldenballs campaign' appealing to its readers for financial contributions, not only for the legal fees, but effectively to guarantee the future of the magazine. The response brought in some unexpected contributors, including several enemies of Goldsmith. The millionaire businessman Tiny Rowland, sent £5,000 and as the campaign snowballed it produced a widespread feeling of dislike for

Goldsmith. Almost overnight, through what appeared like vindictiveness, Goldsmith was showing signs of losing any popularity he might have ever had.

It also lost him what one biographer called the 'congenial anonymity of the rich' which he so enjoyed. Warned by his lawyers that his opponents would be certain to exploit the eccentricities of his private life he decided to pre-empt them. Once more he relied upon his old friend and ally, the *Evening Standard* Paris correspondent Sam White who, from his eyrie in the Crillon bar, wrote about 'James Goldsmith, the man with two families.'

While all this was adding to what Dr Johnson called 'the public stock of harmless pleasure', it became a trial of endurance between Goldsmith and Ingrams. Ingrams finally publicly apologised for libel, and *Private Eye* contributed £30,000 towards Goldsmith's infinitely greater legal costs, but Richard Ingrams's nose and ears had not been cropped, nor was he languishing in prison.

As for Goldsmith, whatever hopes he'd had of avenging his father's humiliation by proudly entering politics in Harold Wilson's government were over, although it seems as if he very nearly made it. On 19 May 1976 the front-page headline in the *Daily Express* proclaimed something that would have made everything worthwhile: 'IT'S LORD GOLDSMITH'. But, not for the first time, the *Express* was mistaken.

What had hapened was that Harold Wilson was bowing out of politics, and helped by Lady Falkender, who had written out the names of his candidates for his 'resignation honours' on lavender paper, had included James Goldsmith, for a peerage. However the Scrutiny Committee, which vets all nominations for peerages, turned him down. Instead he got a knighthood for reasons which were never very clear. His citation states that his knighthood was awarded for 'services to exports and ecology'.

By the time the case ended in 1977, it was clear that for Goldsmith the *Private Eye* affair had become an unmitigated disaster. After hubris comes nemesis. Ivan Fallon was a relatively sympathetic biographer to Goldsmith, but his judgement on the case was unrelenting. 'It changed Goldsmith's image indelibly,' he wrote, 'from that of a businessman with a clever mind, and an immense capacity for making money, into that of an obsessive, angry right-winger, determined to curb the freedom of the British press.'

It also marked the final breakup of the Clermont Set, which had begun so happily nearly twenty years before. Goldsmith, following his father by effectively leaving England rather than making a name in English politics, started a new career and business life abroad. It proved immensely lucrative, but it was also very different from the one he planned before his old friend Lucky Lucan murdered Sandra Rivett.

Epilogue

WITH ONE OF its first five members a murderer and another a suicide, the Clermont Set collapsed, and the three survivors, John Aspinall, James Goldsmith and Mark Birley, followed very different paths in the years ahead.

Goldsmith spent more time than ever now in France, and as so often in the past, he turned once more to gambling, and doing what he did best – playing the markets, mounting financial takeovers on the largest scale, and rarely failing. But the election of a socialist president, his *bête noire*, François Mitterand, in 1981, convinced him that France, like Britain, was unsympathetic to his business interests, and from then on he would be working increasingly from New York. By the mid-eighties he was spending more than half the year in the affluent headquarters he created for himself out of a pair of old brownstone houses beside Central Park.

The rest of his time was spent between Cole Porter's old house on the Rue Monsieur in Paris with Ginette and his French family, and Ormeley Lodge the splendid Queen Anne house at Petersham in Surrey which he bought for Annabel with her and his English family. But it was his business activities in America which would form the culmination of the gambling career that started all those years before at Eton, Oxford and the Clermont.

Goldsmith's complex and immensely profitable dealings on Wall Street during the late eighties and early nineties were the high spot of a period of casino capitalism, and during the rip-roaring, no-holds-barred years of the Reaganite economy, he earned a reputation as 'King of the Corporate Raiders' by launching a series of immensely profitable takeover bids on a number of profoundly rich, diverse and dangerously complacent corporations. This was dealing on a stratospheric level, with billions of dollars sometimes on the table, and none but the coolest, most experienced of gamblers would have had the stamina and nerve to stay the pace. Goldsmith, with a lifetime of successful gambling behind him, ran rings around his opponents, and with his two most spectacular coups – against the vast timber-owning conglomerate Diamond International and the even larger industrial and property-owning corporation Crown Zellerbach – he effectively 'broke the bank', amassing a fortune conservatively estimated at something over three billion dollars in the process.

Although he would overreach himself in his final game, the thirteen billion dollar takeover bid he organised in July 1989 against the massive British American Tobacco Corporation, one might have thought that by then he had amassed a sufficient fortune to satisfy even his 'addictive love of luxury'.

But win or lose, no real gambler is ever satisfied as long as the game continues, and since gambling was still what mattered to James Goldsmith, his private life remained as complex and involved as ever. Although he was a lifelong womaniser, the fact that most women are by nature too sensible and conscious of the practicalities of life to make successful gamblers meant that, however irresistible he found them, he never quite regarded them as equals. And since he was now so rich and powerful, he found no difficulty treating his women and his separate families exactly as he wanted.

In 1978 in what might be termed 'a divorce of convenience', he ended his marriage to the long-suffering Ginette (while assuring her that this would change nothing in her status and their relationship) and finally marrried Annabel, who was forty-five and had been his mistress for fourteen years, in order to legitimise their children, Jemima, Zachariah and Benjamin.

In his one recorded wisecrack, Goldsmith once remarked that, 'When a man marries his mistress, he creates a job vacancy.' This time the successful applicant turned out to be Laure Boulay de la Meurthe, a twenty-eight-year-old journalist and niece of the Comte de Paris, pretender to the throne of France. After making her his mistress, Goldsmith made no attempt to hide the situation from either Annabel or Ginette.

Strong-willed woman that she was, Annabel made her feelings clear, but her husband took remarkably little notice and with the sexual assurance which only the possession of very large amounts of money can confer, he set up home with Laure quite openly in the double house by Central Park, and was soon starting yet another family with the birth of their daughter, Charlotte, in 1983. She was followed by Goldsmith's eighth and final child, his son Jethro, born in 1987. In the words of one journalist, 'like a lion he enjoys a pride of wives.'

With three families and all the money he could ever want, Goldsmith should have been a very happy man, but his superstitions and his bouts of pessimistic melancholy grew with the years. His brother, ecology-obsessed Teddy, was convinced that mankind was hell-bent on imminent destruction, and the idea gradually obsessed him too. He already had a perfect European hideaway in the château of Montjeu near Dijon, one of the great houses of France whose formal gardens and grandiose apartments were the work of Le Nôtre, architect of Louis XIV's Palace of Versailles, which Montjeu resembled; but even this was not enough. During the early nineties, much of his energy and wealth were spent creating what he hoped would be his ultimate redoubt, a private Shangri-La called Cuixmala, constructed in the depths of two thousand acres of tropical forest in the Yucatán peninsula of Mexico. The central building had a gilded dome supposedly copied from the Taj Mahal. Over two hundred servants were in residence to cater for a hundred guests in total luxury. If there was anything a guest desired which wasn't there already, it would be flown in at once from Europe or New York. The real purpose of the house, however, lay in the large bomb-proof shelter, complete with underground supplies and an independent power source that would enable its owner and his family to survive even a nuclear disaster.

★

One of the most frequent visitors to Cuixmala was the man who was still Goldsmith's oldest and firmest friend, John Aspinall. The original relationship between these two great gamblers had changed. It was now Goldsmith, not Aspinall, who was the all-powerful silverback gorilla, lording it over the creatures of the jungle. As we have seen, it was thanks to Goldsmith that Aspinall survived the Wall Street Crash of 1974, and it was also thanks to Goldsmith that he made a second fortune six years later when Goldsmith financed him to start a small gambling club just behind Harrod's in Knightsbridge. Gradually the old magic seemed to work, and three years later, still entirely with Goldsmith's backing, Aspinall moved into the house in Curzon Street which had once been the Curzons' town house. The club, Aspinall's, flourished as the Clermont had before it, so much so that in 1987 he sold it for £90 million, half of which went to him and half to Goldsmith. Finding himself a multi-millionaire for the second time in his life, Aspinall proceeded to place the capital in charitable trusts to support Howletts and the secondary zoo he had founded at Port Lympne.

Although this meant that as with Goldsmith, his financial cares were now behind him, age was beginning to exaggerate his increasingly pessimistic view of life. With just a few exceptions he preferred his animals to human beings and made no secret of his hatred of what he called the 'urban biomass' of less opulent humanity. He saw little to his liking in the way the world was going, and like Teddy Goldsmith was convinced that the planet was in dire straits from overpopulation. He enjoyed shocking the unwary by remarking, with total seriousness, that he'd be 'very happy to see more than 3.5 billion humans wiped off the face of the earth.'

Since rarely a day still passed without Goldsmith and Aspinall talking on the telephone, it was not surprising that, as a pair of passionate Cold War Warriors, they also shared equally pessimistic attitudes to world politics. This particularly applied to Africa, where Aspinall now had an interest since he and his wife Sally had bought yet another large house and estate near Cape Town in South Africa. In the early nineties with the fight against apartheid coming to the boil, Aspinall pinned all his hopes, not on what he and Goldsmith regarded as the communist-dominated African National Congress of Mandela, but on their bitter rivals, Aspinall's boyhood heroes, the Zulus of Natal.

The fact that a bloody war was going on between the ANC and the Zulus of the Inkatha party did not worry them. Aspinall still shared the dreams of Rider Haggard's hero Alan Quartermain, who in retirement had still longed to see 'the Zulu impis breaking on their foes like surf on the rocks.' For Aspinall, Chief Buthelezi, the Inkatha leader, was the reincarnation of his boyhood hero, Shaka, King of the Zulus, and Aspinall caused considerable surprise by arriving at an Inkatha rally. After assuring them 'I am a white Zulu', he urged them 'to sharpen their spears' and use them on their enemies in the ANC.

Between them Aspinall and Goldsmith contributed more than £1 million to what they regarded as heroic fighters for the Zulu nation. Much of this money undoubtedly went to pay for what would now be called acts of terrorism, including sabotage and assassinations against the ANC. The most charitable view that one can take of their actions was that they saw them as part of a romantic game in which they played the part of Rider Haggard heroes against the forces of destruction and disorder.

*

By the early nineteen nineties James Goldsmith's love of risk and extravagant financial deals had placed him among the dozen or so richest human beings on the planet, and although by now he'd won so much that there was little point in gambling further, even the most successful gambler knows that there is still an unseen player waiting who always wins the final round. Just as his old friend Lucan had once 'gambled with his life', Goldsmith now began to do the same.

He hated the idea of death, not from fear of

dying, but because Death could deprive him of his winnings. This had already made him a dedicated hypochondriac and in 1995, when he discovered he had liver cancer, Aspinall convinced him that his best hope of survival was through a strict control of diet, and avoidance of conventional medical treatment, painkillers included. He stoically followed Aspinall's advice, kept all his wits about him and continued with this final gamble he was playing. Even in early 1997, when the cancer reached his pancreas, it did not shake his faith, either in his Indian healer nor in the strict regime that he prescribed.

Not long before his death this king of gamblers embarked on his final coup. By now he knew, of course, that Death was winning and would soon be calling in his bet, but even so there remained one side bet that was worth taking. Being a realist, Goldsmith made careful plans in case Death caught him unawares.

By July when it was clear his days were numbered, he retired to Montjeu, where Ginette was waiting for him with their children Manes and Alix, and his daughter Isabel. Although he had been divorced from Ginette for nearly twenty years, they remained close friends. With death approaching he wanted her support as he bade farewell to their children. But he had no intention of dying in Montjeu.

To die in France would have made him liable to heavy death duties. To avoid them, he had carefully arranged that when his sickness reached its final phase, he would be driven by ambulance to the airport at Toulouse where his private Boeing 727 would be waiting, fuelled and ready to fly him at a moment's notice to Málaga in Spain. From there he would be taken on by helicopter, so that he could spend his final hours in yet another of his splendid residences, the villa in the hills above Marbella which he had recently made over to Annabel.

By dying he would of course be yielding the final game to Death. That was inevitable, but by dying in Spain and not in France, he would at least have won that side bet against the French tax authorities. He had arranged for Annabel to be waiting for him there, but she would not be on her own. The scene required the presence of the other key performer. Annabel must be accompanied by his mistress, Laure Boulaye de la Meurthe.

Thus he could die at peace in this house which he loved, comforted not only by his English wife, but also by his younger and devoted French mistress. At the same time this lifelong gambler, by dying in Spain instead of France, would win for his estate something over sixty million dollars. On 19 July 1997 James Goldsmith had a second major heart attack which killed him.

Aspinall himself succumbed to cancer three years later. Shortly before he died, he and his wife Sally were attacked by muggers while in London. In spite of the fact that he had only just emerged from hospital after a serious operation on his jaw, he tried to fight them off, but was badly hurt. He never really recovered from the attack. Like Goldsmith, he shunned painkillers almost to the last.

Among the last to visit him were two of his closest primate friends – Henry Kissinger and Lord (Conrad) Black, the owner of the *Daily Telegraph*, who arrived simultaneously to pay one last farewell.

It was during the week before he died that he finally made peace with his eldest son, Damian, who maintained that he had had a deeply unhappy childhood, with his father showing him little or no affection, because all his love was showered on his animals But by now, by his own efforts, Damian had ammassed a large fortune in the London property market. Because of this, Aspinall felt that Damian was the one person he could trust to carry on his life's work and appointed him his heir.

One night, shortly before his death, as Damian sat by his bedside, Aspinall finally apologised for his shortcomings as a father, in the only way he knew. It was a scene reminiscent of his behaviour at the bedside of young Robin Birley all those years before. According to Damian. 'My father started kissing my cheek and stroking my face and gurgling in gorilla language. There was no real conversation but I knew that he was saying sorry.'

★

If there is a moral to this story of the five members of the Clermont Circle, it has to be that by the nature of the game even the most successful gamblers end up losing. Clearly, both Lucan and Elwes had been natural losers from the start, but even Goldsmith, who was probably the most successful gambler of our time, lost in the end.

None of his enormous winnings brought what he really wanted. He left behind no lasting achievements commensurate with his fortune – no dynasty like the Rothschilds, no great art collection or museum named after him like Thyssen and Jean Paul Getty, and certainly no public reputation as a philanthropist, like Andrew Carnegie or Rockefeller. Today the great Mogul palace which he built in Yucatán is overgrown with tropical vegetation, and no one, including Isabel who owns it, seems to know quite what to do with it. His final effort to finance a hundred anti-European candidates for his Referendum Party in the 1997 British General Election, produced not a solitary success, nor did he leave behind an enduring business empire. His children by Annabel live essentially private lives: Jemima's marriage to the cricketer Imran Khan, did not last, Zac has taken over his uncle Teddy's magazine, *Ecology*, and Benjamin married a Rothschild in September 2003. His son, Manes, manages a football team in Mexico.

*

Out of the five members of the original Clermont Set, only Mark Birley, the sole survivor, urbane and elegant as ever, can be seen as something of a winner. But then, thanks to that mysterious row he had with Aspinall all those many years before, he was a gambler no longer. Instead, like Candide who survived the horrors of his time and went off to 'cultivate his garden', he continued to cultivate his restaurants, like 'Mark's' and Harry's Bar and his last creation, the dining club that he called 'George'.

He did so with his customary shrewdness, using the expertise that he acquired when creating Annabel's, and catering for the needs of the new super-rich who were making London the most expensive capital in Europe.

It was always much the same formula – exclusivity, and not so much sex now as a search for the absolute perfection which he had been pursuing all his life. He has handed recently on Annabel's and his other clubs to his son Robin and his daughter India Jane who now run them.

Mark himself never remarried, but tragedy did strike him and Annabel in 1984 when their eldest son Rupert disappeared while swimming off a particularly dangerous beach in West Africa. This was something from which neither he nor Annabel ever fully recovered.

Today he still lives in considerable style and luxury in a mansion in the heart of Kensington. In his dressing room he obsessively keeps all his old ties, suits and hand made shoes, as mementoes of happier days gone by. In the same way he has kept in close touch with Annabel over the years. Now with Jimmy and Aspinall both gone, it is almost as if the past had never been. Mark and Annabel often dine together and seem devoted to each other. As great survivors they have much in common and much to talk about.

Postscript

The Ultimate Gamble

Although this ends the story of the Clermont Set, much of the mystery around the fate of the 7th Earl of Lucan persists. The hush-up following the crime was so complete, and so many years have passed that, barring a most unlikely death-bed confession from somebody involved – perhaps even shadowy Mr. X himself – we will never know all the details surrounding Lucky's most unlucky death.

But this does not prevent us piecing together what facts we have about this most absorbing crime, and deciding beyond readonable doubt, what happened to the homicidal earl. With hindsight one can see that Lucan was a dead man from the moment he killed Sandra Rivett by mistake, and thereby lost the wager he had made, to win back his children. From this moment, his one real hope of saving his own skin would have been to have given himself up to the police, trusting in the law to take whatever cause it did.

Instead, by opting to escape, and relying on various friends to help him, Lucan turned himself into an outlaw as well as a murderer, dependant on others for his safety. It was an unenviable situation even for a murderer. It was also one in which his danger would have actually increased as time passed, and the hazards of the situation dawned on everyone involved.

So, who were these 'friends' who assisted Lucan to escape? Apart from Susie Maxwell-Scott's unsubstantiated statement about Mr. X, there is no first-hand evidence of anybody else. And whoever they were, they left the scene of the escape as clean and anonymous as they found it.

Despite this, it is not too difficult to work out who masterminded the escape, by a simple process of elimination. Indeed the personal requirements demanded for this role were so specific and demanding, that one man and one alone among Lucan's friends clearly possessed them all.

First and foremost, he must have been a close and a devoted friend of the murderer. No one else in his right mind would have got involved with somebody who telephoned at night demanding help after a murder had gone so spectacularly wrong. Secondly, he must have already had a fairly good idea of the murderer's intentions, to have been able to mount that night's instant operation which saved Lucan from arrest. Then, he must have sympathised with Lucan's original plan to kill his wife, however disastrously it turned out. And finally he must have had compelling reasons of his own to keep his friend Lucan out of the hands of the police.

All of this applies to Aspinall. He also had the nerve, the cool self-confidence and the decisiveness needed in this sort of crisis. The excitement of the situation would have appealed to his taste for living dangerously; and a man who believed in culling several million of the world's surplus population, would have felt few qualms about one bungled murder.

These remarks he made to Lyn Barber some years later are particularly revealing. Yes, he did believe that a man was justified in murdering his wife if she provoked him and gave him little alternative.' And he made it very clear that he would have helped his 'great friend' Lucan, despite knowing he was a murderer, because he was in a 'terrible position', and 'a friend is needed when things are going badly'.

All of which makes it clear beyond reasonable doubt that it was John Aspinall who helped Lucan to escape on that November night in 1974. It's also clear that whatever rumours Aspinall fed to the police to put them off the scent, Lucan did not kill himself by jumping from a power-boat into the Solent. There was no power-boat, and Lucan, as Aspinall knew quite well, never had been suicidal. Besides, the letter he wrote to Michael Stoop about his car, the day following his disappearance, proves that he was still alive till then.

Aspinall would have had little difficulty finding a temporary safe haven for Lucan somewhere along the coast. But with the police soon to be searching for him in the homes of fellow gamblers and friends, he had to be got away from England fast.

There is no reason to doubt Susie Maxwell Scott's word for it that Aspinall's friendly fence and money launderer, Mr. X, helped smuggle Lucan from the country and ensured that he was kept firmly under wraps abroad. This sort of work was not for amateurs, and the absolute discretion with which Lucan disappeared suggests the involvement of a true professional with access to equally professional accomplices from the European underworld who could be entirely trusted.

Up to this point everyone involved in Lucan's disappearance would have been hoping to keep him out of the hands of the police until the hue and cry died down, and arrangements could be made to build him a new life in another country. In theory, at least, this could have happened. If not James Goldsmith, then some other risk-addicted multi-millionaire might well have been persuaded to finance what would have been an expensive and on-going exercise in deception. Lucan could have been transferred to a discreet cosmetic clinic in, say, Switzerland, given a new face and a fresh identity, and the world just might have been his oyster.

But nobody, however rich or reckless, would have taken the appalling risk of financing a murderer like Lucan who was in the middle of a nervous crisis, obsessed with proving his innocence and longing to be one day reunited with his children. Thanks to the interest in the case being whipped up in the media, Lucan had become the most wanted man in the world, and as long as he remained alive, neither Aspinall, nor any of those Clermont friends, who had got themselves involved, were ever going to sleep soundly in their beds. Nor, for that matter, could anyone employed to look after Lucan since his flight.

It is this that brings us to the crux of Lucan's fate. However kind and disinterested his motives, anyone who gets involved in helping a wanted man escape becomes complicit in his crime. Too late in the day the Kray Twins realised this sobering truth after freeing their friend, 'The Mad Axeman,' Frank Mitchell, from Dartmoor, and concealing him in a basement flat in Stoke Newington. As soon as Mitchell started acting up, thus threatening them with serious trouble with the police, they saw no alternative but to have him killed – and promptly did so.

In a way, the situation facing Lucan's minders was worse than Mitchell's. Mitchell was a simple-minded thug, but Lucan had murdered an innocent woman in cold blood, and anyone caught helping him evade arrest had real problems. Since we know that Lucan was not suicidal, and far too many people would have been at risk had he ever been let loose with a fresh identity, there can be only one conclusion. After what undoubtedly involved much agonising discussion somebody, somewhere exercised what might be termed 'The Axeman Option.' Unless Lord Lucan died of natural causes, someone must have killed him.

Perhaps Susie Maxwell-Scott was right and the murderer's murderer was Mr X, but her word for this apart, there is no proof of this. From what I know of Mr X, I'd not have thought that murder was his line, and he'd have been far more likely to have got someone else to do the deed. Even then he would never have arranged to have had Lucan killed without being given orders to do so.

One of the characters in Eric Ambler's classic thriller, 'The Mask of Demetrios', remarks that 'what really matters is not who pulled the trigger, but who paid for the bullets'. This is the question that remains at the heart of the death of the 7th Earl of Lucan.

Interestingly, the answer lies in the one feature that runs like a connecting thread through the tangled background of this whole strange story – gambling. Just as Lucan's plan to murder Lady Lucan became virtually an in-house crime at the Clermont, so we have Aspinall's own word for it that he and Lucan really did regard the whole 'adventure' as a legitimate gamble. Other members of the Clermont seem to have done the same. And, as we have seen, some years later, Aspinall was still seeing the whole murder plan as such a memorable wager that it qualified Lucan for a place in his pantheon of the greatest gamblers of all time. He must have had his moments of remorse, and this would have been one way of settling a debt of honour.

That was as maybe, but the point about the greatest gamble of Lord Lucan's life was that he lost. Aspinall and Lucan belonged to the unforgiving brotherhood of addicted high-stakes gamblers, and both of them knew the score. As dedicated gamblers both had lived their lives according to a code which makes it clear that if you gamble and you lose there can be no argument. You pay the price.

By staking his life to gain his children, Lucan had made his ultimate gamble with death itself. Since he'd lost, and his continued presence was now endangering his friends and fellow gamblers, the time had come for someone to ensure the debt was honoured.

In this situation, there was one person, and one

alone, with the nerve and expertise to do this. Enforcing gambling debts was part of Aspinall's profession. He had never shrunk from painful decisions when they were inevitable, nor would he have let sentimental arguments about the sanctity of human life cloud his judgement. As a gambler himself, Lucky would also have seen the justice of what was happening and understood that, although he was his friend, Aspinall had no alternative. Besides, it would have been beneath Aspinall's dignity not to have ensured payment of the most sensational bet of his career, just as it would have been beneath Lucky's to have expected to be let off. Whoever may have pulled the trigger, I think we know who paid for the bullets.

Bibliography

Al Alvarez *The Biggest Game in Town*

John Ashton *The History of Gambling in England*

John Aspinall *The Best of Friends*

David Cannadine *The Decline and Fall of the British Aristocracy*

Annabel Davis-Goff *The Literary Companion to Gambling*

Dominick Elwes and Nicholas Luard *Refer to Drawer*

Ivan Fallon *Billionaire*

Frederick Foreman *Respect*

David Gerring (w. Robert Brimmell) *Lucan Lives*

Annabel Goldsmith *Annabel*

Charles Graves *None but the Rich*

John Halliday and Peter Fuller (ed.) *The Psychology of Gambling*

bibliography

Cheis Nutchins and Dominic Midgley *Goldsmith: Money, Women and Power*

Richard Ingrams *Goldenballs*

Norman Lucas *The Lucan Mystery*

Brian Masteres *The Passion of John Aspinall*

Scutator *The Odds at Monte Carlo*

Geoffrey Wansell *Tycoon: The Life of James Goldsmith*

List of Illustrations

Antenor Patino, 1st February 1955 © Evening Standard/Getty Images.
The Duchess of Durcal, Christina Patino © Toppfoto.co.uk.
James Goldsmith and his wife Isabelle Patina © Carl Mydans/Time Life Pictures/Getty Images.
James Goldsmith with his daughter Isabella and a nurse in Paris, 9th October 1954 © Grace Robertson/Picture Post/Getty Images.
Newly-weds, Mark Birley and his wife the former Lady Annabel Vane-Tempest-Stewart, 10th March 1954 © Topfoto.co.uk.
The Maxwell-Scott wedding.
John Aspinall, 9th January 1958 © Reg Davis/Express/Getty Images.
John Aspinall and his wife ex-model Jane with

their pet monkey 'Dead Loss', 11th January 1958 © Keystone/Getty Images.

Dominick Elwes and Tessa Kennedy after their elopement to Cuba, 5th Feburary 1958 © Topfoto.co.uk.

The Clermont Club, 44 Berkeley Square W1 © Topfoto.co.uk.

John Aspinall plays with tigers at his private zoo, July 3rd 1971 © Hulton-Deutsch Collections/CORBIS.

Richard John Bingham, Earl of Lucan and Veronica Duncan after their marriage, 28th November 1963 © Douglas Miller/Keystone/Getty Images.

John Aspinall leaving with his second wife Belinda Musker after their wedding, December 13th 1966 © Topfoto.co.uk.

John Aspinall and his third wife Lady Sarah (Sally) Aspinall and tiger cubs, August 1971 © Mirrorpix.

Dominick Elwes and Helen Jay. Property of Helen Pennant-Ray ©. Reproduced by kind permission.

James Goldsmith and his partner Lady Annabel Birley arrive at Bow Street Court, 29th July 1976 © Central Press/Getty Images.

Dominick Elwes and John Aspinall. Property of Helen Pennant-Ray ©. Reproduced by kind permission.

Dominick Elwes on horseback. Property of Helen Pennant-Ray ©. Reproduced by kind permission.

Veronica Lucan, wife of the missing Earl, Lord Lucan. 15th November 1974 © Frank Barratt/Keystone/Getty Images.

Sir James Goldsmith with his family, 1st August 1987 © Peter Jordan/Time Life Pictures/Getty Images.

Sir James Goldsmith, on the campaign trail. 8th April 1997 © Polak Matthew/CORBIS.

Lady Annabel Goldsmith and ex-husband, Mark Birley, 16th September 2003 © Mark Stewart/Camera Press.

Index

index

index

index

index

index

index

One of the Family

John Pearson

John Pearson's *The Profession of Violence* created the myth of the Kray twins, and remains a classic of true crime, the best book ever written on East London villains and a book that started a mini publishing industry.

Pearson knows the London crime scene as well as anyone, which is why he was surprised while attending Ronnie Kray's funeral to see a man to whom all the other villains deferred, but whom he didn't recognize. Investigation revealed that this man, the Englishman, never mentioned in any of the previous books on villainy because everyone was too scared to mention his name, was as legendary a figure on the streets of New York as on the streets of London. Pearson persuaded him to talk to him – and the result was a story even more extraordinary than that of the Krays. He became the adopted son of Joey Pagano, the head of one of the major New York crime families. Here the Englishman tells the story that no-one else dared to tell.

arrow books

On the Run

Gregg and Gina Hill

By the son and daughter of Henry Hill – immortalised in the Martin Scorsese film *Goodfellas* – *On The Run* – is the harrowing account of a childhood spent coping with an explosive father whilst dodging Mafia payback.

Henry Hill's business partner, Jimmy Burke has whacked every person who could possibly implicate him in the infamous Lufthansa robbery at JFK airport. On his way to prison, lifelong ganster Henry is given two options: sleep with the fishes, or enter the FBI's Witness Protection Program. Gregg and Gina are dragged along for the ride. Like nomads, they're forced to wander from state to state, constantly inventing new names and finding new friends, only to abandon them at a moment's notice. Living under constant fear of being found and killed.

But Henry, the rock Gregg and Gina so desperately need, is a heavy cocaine user and knows only the criminal life. He is soon up to his old tricks and consistently putting their identities in jeopardy. The kids, can no longer ignore that the Mob might be less of a threat to them than remaining under the roof of their increasingly unbalanced father.

'An extraordinary story' Julie Gregory, author of *Sickened*

arrow books

ALSO AVAILABLE IN ARROW

The Badge

Jack Webb

There has been no other epoch in American history where corruption, debauchery, sleaze and horrific murder has intersected with a society as speciously glittering and innocent as the Los Angeles of the 1940s and 50s.

The Tinseltown of that age had movie star glamour on the surface but a dark, violent and unrepentant heart. None knew this dichotomy better than the Los Angeles Police Department, whose story became the most successful police drama in television history, *Dragnet*. Jack Webb was the star and creator of the show, but much of what he unearthed was too sensational to be broadcast on prime time. Those stories he saved for his classic, *The Badge*.

Crimes like the sex slaying of Betty Short, the Black Dahlia: tortured for days, drained of blood, cut in two and dumped in Leimert Park, the subject of James Ellroy's masterpiece and one of the US's greatest unsolved murders. Narcotics, gambling, prostitution, thrill murders, serial killers – all take their place in a book that shattered America's delusion of post-war innocence and defines our knowledge of modern crime even today.

arrow books

Philip & Elizabeth

Gyles Brandreth

This is the first biography of the Queen and the Duke of Edinburgh – both royal, both great-great-grandchildren of Queen Victoria, but, in temperament and upbringing, two very different people. The Queen's childhood was loving and secure, the Duke's was turbulent: his grandfather assassinated, his father arrested, his family exiled, his parents separated when he was only ten.

Elizabeth and Philip met as cousins in the 1930s. They married in 1947, aged twenty-one and twenty-six. A little more than four years later, they were Queen and consort. For almost sixty years theirs have been among the most famous faces in the world – yet the personalities behind the image remain elusive and the nature of their marriage is an enigma.

Philip & Elizabeth tells the extraordinary story of these two contrasting lives, assesses their achievement, together and apart, and explores the nature of their relationships, with one another and with their children.

arrow books

ALSO AVAILABLE IN ARROW

Charles & Camilla
Gyles Brandreth

This is the definitive account of one of the most extraordinary stories of our time. Gyles Brandreth, acclaimed biographer of the Queen and Prince Philip, presents a unique portrait of their son, Charles, Prince of Wales, and of the one 'non-negotiable' love of his life, Camilla Shand, now Duchess of Cornwall.

What are Charles and Camilla really like? What is their heritage? What has made them the way they are? This is both a revealing portrait of two unusual individuals and a family saga like no other, told with unrivalled authority and insight – and humour – by a best-selling writer who has met all the key characters in the drama: Charles, Camilla, Diana, their children, their families and their friends.

'Could this be the best book ever written about the Royal Family? . . . A masterpiece.' *Sunday Express*

'Utterly fascinating' Andrew Marr, *Start the Week*

'Highly accomplished . . . there is much here to entertain and inform' *Sunday Telegraph*

'Completely fascinating – written by the man who really knows' Richard Madeley, *Richard and Judy*

arrow books

A Likely Story

Rodney Bewes

By turns funny, charming and sad, this is the story of a sensitive and sickly lad's northern working-class childhood and subsequent rise to fame. Along the way, we hear of his laddish behaviour in swinging London in the company of the biggest stars of the day, including how he climbed Big Ben to hang a pair of knickers on the hand of the clock; of his troubled relationship with Likely Lads co-star James Bolam; and many celebrity stories, featuring Ralph Richardson, Laurence Olivier, Rod Steiger, Tom Courtney and Raquel Welch. *A Likely Story* is everything you would expect from the autobiography of a moon-struck clown.

'In his cheerfully outrageous memoirs, he reveals a comic touch every bit as sharp as the show's scriptwriters.'
Daily Mail

arrow books

Said and Done

Roger McGough

Roger McGough is one of Britain's best-loved poets, whose humour, distinctive voice, and sharp eye for the idiosyncrasies of everyday life, have made him a household name. Since enjoying overnight success with The Scaffold, whose song Lily the Pink reached the number one spot worldwide, he has moved in a seemingly contradictory world where poetry coexists with comedy and pop music, becoming one of the leading lights of British poetry for children and adults alike.

Like the best of his poetry, his autobiography is packed with humour, honesty, surreal observations, nostalgic reminiscences and poignant, bittersweet tales of love, life and loss.

'Delightfully self-deprecating autobiography . . . his prose is lovely, considered, concise and frequently frivolous, but it never strays far from the poetry that is his natural environment and, essentially, his subject'
The Independent on Sunday

'A warm-hearted book about the extraordinary life of an extraordinary man. He may choose to depict himself as Mr Ordinary, but there is nothing at all ordinary about his energy or talent' *Independent*

arrow books

ALSO AVAILABLE IN ARROW

The Lost Life of Eva Braun

Angela Lambert

Eva Braun is one of history's most famous nonentities. Yet fifty-eight years after her death her name is still instantly recognisable.

After leaving convent school at the age of seventeen, she became Hitler's mistress before she was twenty. How did unsophisticated little Fräulein Braun, twenty-three years his junior, hold the most powerful man in Europe in an exclusive sexual relationship that lasted until their joint suicide? This authoritative biography, explores how, living at the cold heart of the Nazi leadership, she could have beengenuinely ignorant of the atrocities of the Third Reich.

'Lambert combines her knowledge of culture . . . with her novelist's sensibility to drive to the heart of this dark and unpalatable puzzle' *Guardian*

'A highly readable account . . . [it] admirably fulfils its brief of rescuing its subject both from Hitler's shadow and the charges of hostile witnesses' *Daily Mail*

'Lambert has written an interesting book about her [Eva] and her still horribly absorbing period' *Independent on Sunday*

'Lively and readable biography' *Sunday Times*

arrow books